Praise for *Forms of Feeling*

"How is it possible to live, in this culture at this moment, a life filled with poetry? John Morgan's essays, meditations, and interviews answer that: like this, like this, like this. Morgan takes us from his student days at Harvard and Iowa to his days as professor emeritus, the span of a life lived in lines, a life of poetry. When the most critical challenges occur, like the terrible illness of a child, Morgan shows how vital precise language can be. Precisely located, mostly in Alaska, this prose is life-giving, grounded and smart."

PEGGY SHUMAKER
author of *Gnawed Bones* and *Just Breathe Normally*

"John Morgan's finely wrought and delightful new book is by turns meditative, confessional, instructional—even cajoling (on behalf of poetry). In the examined life of this thoughtful poet, readers will find solace and meaning and entertainment too."

DAN O'NEILL
author of *A Land Gone Lonesome* and *The Firecracker Boys*

Forms of Feeling

Poetry in Our Lives. Essays & Interviews

JOHN MORGAN

For Donald Wesling,
With warm wishes,
John Morgan

salmonpoetry

Published in 2012 by
Salmon Poetry
Cliffs of Moher, County Clare, Ireland
Website: www.salmonpoetry.com
Email: info@salmonpoetry.com

ISBN 978-1-907056-91-8

COVER ARTWORK: *Judy Orvik*
COVER DESIGN: *Siobhán Hutson*

for Nancy:
> *in this age of*
> *war and purchased love*
> *mine's a free answer*

Acknowledgements

Earlier versions of these essays, articles and interviews originally appeared in the following publications:

ALASKA, REFLECTIONS ON LAND AND SPIRIT (The University of Arizona Press): "Letter from Wales (Alaska)"

THE ASSOCIATED WRITING PROGRAMS NEWSLETTER (now WRITER'S CHRONICLE): "Suspension of Disbelief" and "Revision Means Seeing Again"

THE FAIRBANKS DAILY NEWS-MINER: "National Poetry Month"

49WRITERS.COM: "An Interview with John Morgan," "Firstlings," "Denali Park Journal," and "Robert Lowell Remembered"

FOURTH GENRE: "The Dig at Polecat Bench, 1961"

MĀNOA: "Season of Dead Water" and "Tales from the Dena"

THE NORTH AMERICAN REVIEW: "Letter from Fairbanks" and "Letter from Wales (Alaska)"

PERMAFROST: "An Interview with John Morgan"

UNDER NORTHERN LIGHTS (The University of Washington Press): "Moving to Fairbanks: Notes on Poetry and Place"

I would like to thank The Alaska State Council on the Arts, The Rasmuson Foundation, and The Fine Arts Work Center for their generous support. Also thanks to the University of Alaska Fairbanks which facilitated my visit to the remote village of Wales, Alaska, and to the Visiting Artists Program at Denali National Park and Alaska Geographic which supported my residency in the park.

My deepest gratitude to these friends who gave helpful comments and suggestions: Jean Anderson, Burns Cooper, Susheila Khera, John Kooistra, Dan O'Neill, Linda Schandelmeier, and Frank Soos.

Contents

I.

POETRY IN OUR LIVES

NATIONAL POETRY MONTH

You catch a whiff of something on the border of consciousness. A phrase floats into your head and you recognize the voice. A fly buzzes at the windowsill; you wonder what it thinks it's doing. Usually we dismiss such occurrences. They seem to have no practical use. But the suspicion lingers that these events may be trying to tell us something, to point out a meaning that, in the course of our busy lives, we've been too distracted to face. Everyone has such moments, but what do you do with them? What do you make from them? What purpose can they serve?

Robert Frost called the poem, "A momentary stay against confusion," and the poet Greg Orr explains: "We are creatures whose volatile inner lives are both mysterious to us and beyond our control. How to respond to the unpredictability of our own emotional being? One important answer is the personal lyric, the poem dramatizing inner and outer experience."

In other words, poetry gives form to our feelings and helps us come to terms with them. Facing the emotions of a personal crisis, a poem can be the beginning of healing. The crisis may be small or massive—a cut finger or a child in a coma—but in either case poetry is one possible response. The widespread rediscovery of poetry after 9/11 illustrates this point.

But if poetry is good in a crisis, it's also a way of reaching out for new experiences and renewing our lives. Poems place themselves between the world of dream and what we might think of as the prose of reality. Using metaphor, seductive sound and fantastic narrative, poems can evoke mysterious states. When I'm working on a draft, it's this feeling of otherworldliness, no matter how ordinary the subject, that tells me I may have a poem going.

But how do you recognize a poem, when you sense one buzzing around the room? Well, of course there's not just one way to go at poems. A phrase pops into your head, or a rhythm, a mental image, a smell, or sound. Things are always floating into our heads. Usually we brush them aside, but maybe there's a poem there. Even that fly on the windowsill—as in Emily Dickinson's disturbing and wonderful poem, "I heard a fly buzz when I died…"

It's my contention that poems are happening all the time. In a quiet moment, you can cultivate one. I sometimes go out to a spot overlooking the Tanana River near my home in central Alaska and just sit and wait. Soon I'm noticing things that hadn't been apparent at first. And what I see draws new thoughts to mind that I'd been too busy to notice. I step back and start taking mental notes on what I'm seeing, hearing, thinking, and as often as not these things begin working themselves into a poem. Here's an example:

ABOVE THE TANANA: APRIL

for the New Rochelle High Class of '61

A crane, in snow showers, drifts above the river
where, this morning, two jet fighters buzzed

the flats. I look for other signs of life.
A scrap of blue-green color on the ground

turns out to be the wrapper of a half-inch
firecracker. Did Jeffrey—ten next Thursday—

set it off? Last fall (as thought steps back)
at our 25th reunion, Molly, now a writer of romances

seemed old in flashy make-up and long lashes.
We danced in the 9th grade to Buddy Holly

holding close, and once, in nursery school
as I recall, we shed our underpants

to have a look. Now 'Muzzy' (John Mazzulo)
is a medical professor, adamantly gay.

And most bizarre—John Seeman, our
annual class president, still "a real

nice guy", has made himself a star
in porno flicks. But look at me. With hair

down to my shoulders, back east from far
Alaska and a poet—I'm one of the exotics

of the class. We sat on the grass beside
the whitewashed Tom Paine Cottage—kept

as it was by those radical D.A.R.s—and talked
about the ones who weren't there. Steph,

my hopeless crush in the third grade,
dead of a brutal tumor these ten years,

and Andy Miller, 6-2 white point-guard, who
turned to drugs and dealing, and got blown away.

I said we'd put on masks: balding, gray,
and wrinkled "monster" versions of ourselves.

And now banning that thought, knitting
my brows, I spot a spider netting two

spruce bows. What's near at hand grows deeper
in the evening light. Beyond her web

the mountains darken under storms. A crescent moon
flies suddenly among the splotchy clouds. The river's

mud-green current swells under thinning ice.

～

Most poems don't give their full meaning away easily. It can take a week or a month to bring one to completion. I spend some time every day working on a draft, and this daily contact is renewing, as the poem grows and shapes itself. In the course of revision I'm learning from the poem what it really wants to say.

And along with writing poems, I read them. If reading poetry seems hard at first, it's probably because you're out of practice. Like anything else, it gets easier the more you do it. Find an anthology and check out some old favorites. Then read around in the book and see if you can make new discoveries. When you find a poet you like, check in the library for a collection of his or her work.

For some, poetry expresses itself through dance or music, but in its root form, of course it's language. Language that dances. Language that sings. Poems remind us, consciously or not, of our first burblings and vocalizations and the pleasure they gave us as infants. Then came nursery rhymes and the jingles of jump rope and hopscotch. As we grow up, we ask other things from poems, but we should never forget that first sensory intoxication.

That's why, even when it shocks us or brings us close to tears, one underlying theme of every good poem is a celebration of human experience.

WHY I AM NOT A NOVELIST

When I sit down to write a poem, I feel—I have always felt, since adolescence when I began to write them—that I am the final authority. In that mood, I'm as like a god as it's possible to be. I know what's on my mind, after all, better than anyone else. I trust my imagination and count on my native honesty to weed out the bullshit. Why then don't these sterling talents also work for me as a novelist? For a couple of reasons, I believe.

Poets have an undeserved reputation as seducers. Poets are not necessarily great seducers; they are, however, experts at being seduced. The biography of Byron bears out this point. Well, for a time I was seduced by the novel—by the idea of the novel, a large inclusive form, a vast potential audience, big advances, movie rights.

It's a common fantasy, of course, and it even works out that way for some people. I can recall the buzz at Bread Loaf the summer before *The World According to Garp* came out. John Irving and I had been students together at Iowa a decade earlier and his breakthrough into the best-seller big-time, long expected, was now at hand. That's what everyone—visiting agents, editors and fellow fiction writers—felt. Even we poets caught the drift. And so it proved. Then why couldn't the same thing happen for me?

Unfortunately, I was not at my core a novelist. Approaching the form, I was timid. I wanted to be original, but there's a lot of technique to fiction and I suspected I hadn't yet mastered it. What was all this talk about points of view, plot arcs, pacing? I wanted to be sure that what I produced was "okay"—that is, acceptable to others. So already this vast audience I'd imagined was looking over my shoulder qualifying what I wrote. And the editors who read my fiction could sense my hesitancy.

Perhaps someday I'll achieve the authority needed and will return to my two unpublished novels and bring them off. I can't be sure, though, and I've vowed not to go back to them until the day when I am overwhelmed by a sense of vocation, when, all hesitancy mastered, I will be for the novel the "final word" I feel I am when I write poetry.

But hold on a minute—am I really the final word? You see before you no superhero—just an ordinary, striving, fatherly, husbandly figure, trying somewhat bumblingly to make his way, to achieve some measure of stability and happiness in the world.

Then who writes the poetry? Let me admit right away that he is not always present. He—this gifted, self-confident creature—appears maybe only once or twice a month. But what he (or she: remember the Muse) then accomplishes is quite startling. He picks up the scraps and jottings of my ordinary self and transforms them into poetry. Often, I sit at my desk and wait unrewarded, or, growing impatient punch out artless lines, free-associating, imitating, or blatantly stealing material—faking it. Then the poet turns up and finds among the bumbler's scrapheap just the stuff he needs, goes to work, and, with a confident eye and heart, fashions poetry. The work may not be finished in an hour or a day, but once the poet has taken a hand in the matter poetry will result. Till then it's hopeless.

The old-fashioned word for this is inspiration. Psychologists studying the creative process talk about "brainstorms"—periods of intense mental activity, a kind of supercharged state observable in moments of genuine creativity.

Psychologists like to use metaphors from electricity and physics. It seems less mysterious. For our purposes, let's call it inspiration.

Can I invoke it? Or must I simply wait and hope?

Does the poet exist as a separate entity inside me, or is he simply what the bumbler becomes when some new catalytic element is added?

Hard to say. But I do know that this figure, the poet, is present at other times too—not just at the computer. I know him in certain moments of perception when a scene or object is taken in with a mysterious surcharge of feeling, depth of insight, or a special thread of associations. Sometimes in dreams, in memories, or in the act of reverie—even reading a book, for that matter—I may feel his presence and know that a poem is possible. At other times, experiences which I do not recall as having had this surcharge of poetic feeling can acquire it later, when I sit down to write.

I am not describing a mental illness—at least I hope not.

The bumbler, though not outstandingly happy or wise can cope with reasonable efficiency in the everyday world. Yet there would be little to note about him if it weren't for that other, rarer component of his personality. The poet gives him a distinction which he feels he has not earned. Oh, on public occasions, he may take on some of the appearance, the ego, the self-confidence of the poet. He is the bumbler still, but he is proud to represent the poet—to stand in for him, as it were—in this public forum. Too much adulation, however, will get him down. He becomes only too aware of the gap between the bumbler he is and the poet he is taken to be by a naïve and credulous audience. Off-stage he returns to his more comfortable everyday self, somewhat apologetic, somewhat self-effacing.

In traditional rituals, we are told, when the dancer puts on the mask of a god, he becomes the god; there is no pretending, no faking about it. Lacking the authority of these rituals, we moderns must do the best we can. The forces that lie below consciousness are dangerous, not just to the individual but to nations: all our modern rationality has not prevented war, has in fact vastly increased its destructive potential. What is repressed by the rational mind comes back around by its own pre-logical and insidious route and contributes to all the horrors we know from recent history. It is against these forces that the poet, the artist must take a stand: our mission isn't to promote the rationality of war-games, but the poorly understood healing and unifying rituals of art.

Every poet knows there are risks. Courage is required. To live at the higher intensity of art at every moment is a dream, perhaps, but a dangerous one. The system, the nerves can't take it. Many of the poets who've tried it have ended badly. They were the ones, I believe, who hadn't learned to live with their everyday bumbling selves, to accept the rarity of inspiration, its exceptional nature. They wanted to live constantly in its flame and it burned them up.

I have felt this desire too: who hasn't? It's like the wish to sustain the ecstatic throes of an orgasm all through the night and never come down from that high. But we are limited creatures: our bodies are not made for it. We may visit that higher world, but then we must return, hoping that the next visit is not too long postponed. And one function of art is perhaps no more than to give us a glimpse and to record the fact for those who come after that men and women have on occasion been tourists in that realm.

Which brings me to the time-honored connection between writing and drugs. Coleridge was experimenting with opium when he had the vision that became "Kubla Khan" and the French symbolists considered it a writer's job to explore the full range of consciousness available through chemistry. In our own time Ginsberg, Burrows and the other Beats embraced this project with gusto and often published their findings. Back in 1970, with Vietnam still raging, it was appealing to see the counter-culture as an admirable alternative to the materialistic, war-mongering mainstream. But tripping out to the far corners of the mind is not going to be of much use to a writer who can't find his way back.

The slip of pink construction paper in my wallet is marked off in squares, each with a yellowish discoloration where an eye dropper dabbed a splash of the chemical. I'd tried the stuff a couple of weeks before with dramatic results. In almost no time I'd come up with solutions to all of the world's thorniest problems (the cures, as I recall, were peace, love, communes for the enlightened, and the lovely Mozart oboe quartet that accompanied my trip). Then, as the drug's sway deepened and spread, I flipped into a wordless psychedelic state. The living room divided into geometrical shapes and the picture window that looked out on the woods multiplied itself and paraded in a herky-jerky fashion into the room. This was actually quite cool, I felt, as was the flood of bright red and purple fruits and flowers which, in the next phase of my journey, turned the stairs into a succulent cornucopia, as they flowed down from the second floor, filling our loaner house with the rich loamy sensations of fruitfulness and birth.

But then I started to feel a bit queasy and, as if to explain this sensation, a segmented umbilical cord wrapped itself around my abdomen and began to constrict me. Throwing coils around me like a python, it held me pinned to the wicker couch. I couldn't move my arms and legs and it seemed as if my insides were being exposed, like some large animal's in a slaughterhouse, my guts and organs spilling out into the room. And terrified that I hadn't hit bottom yet, I blacked out for a while and woke in confusion, fearing I'd gone mad and might never emerge from this hellish nightmare.

Clinging to the banister with both hands, I dragged myself step by step up to the bedroom and managed to get myself under the covers. It felt like a superhuman feat. Then I passed out again. When Nancy came home I told her what I'd done and described the incredible feelings and sights and the horrible freak-out that followed. She helped me through a shaky night and by morning I was wobbling back toward myself.

Incredibly, a couple of weeks later I took acid again. It was as if I didn't fully trust my first trip and needed to confirm that those extraordinary things had really happened. I figured that being aware of the risks, I'd be able to steer clear of the worst parts, but shortly after swallowing the loaded slip of paper, I knew I'd made a big mistake.

I tried to throw it up, but couldn't. So I sat on the living room couch waiting with dread for the drug to kick in. But then it occurred to me that by bringing the force of my will to bear, I might be able to block out the hallucinations and avoid the specters that seemed to leer at me from just around the corner. With fists clenched and chest constricted, I struggled to hold on to my reason and not to give way to the appalling effects of the drug. I felt jumpy and paranoid, but without any of the euphoria or lunacy of my first trip, and after an hour or two I began to hope I was in the clear.

Then around noon someone knocked at the kitchen door.

Wearing flat-brimmed hats, holstered guns and glittering badges with "Sheriff" and "Deputy Sheriff" on them, two cops demanded to know what I was doing in the house. They'd seen laundry hanging outside, they said, and this place was never occupied in the off-season.

"I...I'm a writer. My uncle owns the house and he's letting us use it for the winter."

They squinted skeptically, as if my story had glaring holes in it. "What's your uncle's name?"

"Irving Kahn."

"There's no car in the driveway. Do you have one?"

"My wife's using it." I decided to keep my answers short. The stress of their visit was pushing me to the edge of my competence. My eyes weren't focusing too well and I could feel vibrations from the suppressed drug sloshing up and down my nerves.

"Where is she?"

"In Bayport. She's a school teacher."

"That's a long commute."

"About an hour. She teaches junior high music." I wondered how wasted I looked and it occurred to me that if they asked for identification, I'd have to fish around in my wallet and the remaining construction paper might fall out and give me away.

So far I'd been talking to the senior sheriff, but now his younger sidekick jumped in. "This place isn't set up for winter that I ever heard of."

"It has a furnace." I opened the door to the basement and turned on the overhead light bulb.

The deputy took a few steps down and came back nodding his head.

"We had some work done on it. We also put in that stove." I pointed across the room. The gleaming white four-burner contrasted with the kitchen's ancient refrigerator and discolored sink. Presumably squatters wouldn't bother to buy a new stove.

"Do you have the receipt?" The sheriff went over for a closer look.

I scrounged around among the bills and correspondence scattered on the kitchen table, but couldn't find it. "It must be in the dining room."

On the sideboard, I spotted the manila envelope where Nancy filed our financial papers. I dumped them out on the table and there it was: "Rothman Appliances, Southold." Marked: "Paid."

They seemed relieved, as though during the course of the interrogation they'd become invested in my story. A young writer, even a flaky one, and his musical wife might be worthy additions to this remote North Fork community. Waving goodbye, they strode down the driveway to the waiting patrol car and as soon as they were out of sight, I flushed the remaining LSD down the toilet.

I'll spare you a post-mortem on those two novels I once wrote. Of course it's difficult for me to forget that four years of my life went into them. Call it a learning process—learning my own limits.

One day a funny thing happened, though. Having shipped the second novel off to my agent, I was sitting at my desk punching out some prose for what I thought was going to be a short story. But as I worked on it, the piece got shorter and shorter, the rhythms more and more like poetry. I hadn't written a poem in quite some time and had no thought of ever doing it again. But all the best intentions in the world could not keep this piece from working itself into lines. A poem:

THE BEHAVIORIST

The angles of his face tend toward dispersion,
his ways are diffident, cold, unendearing,

and you wonder about his childhood:
how early this graceless scion of the gentry
knowing that only his brains would carry him
began to perceive those
gestures and responses by which other people
meet and get acquainted, gestures
which he must study in order to know.

It puzzles you how he managed to court his wife
and what attracted her, whether
it was despair
or the thought that she (more fluent in gesture
and in relationships) would eventually
gain mastership in their house; or was it love?

Probably it was love, and that thought
makes you look again,
noticing the cleavages in his face
unable to soften themselves in any way.

Would she say, "He is not easy to know
but once you know him..."?
Now they have moved to Australia,

and have left behind a cat ("Tiger Lily,"
mother of eight, who has moved into your house
and keeps to herself where the warm air gathers
on the attic stairs). Because of her
you have recalled
the isolation he must live with at every moment
which the rest of us submerge in mere "relationships"
until that time
when charm and spontaneity can do us no more good
and we must cast off, along with our confusions,
the concinnity of features that was our mask.

After that, I found it harder and harder to conceal from myself where I ought to put my effort—not into the large, inclusive and economically viable form—but rather into the diminutive, subjective and unprofitable: in short, I was a poet, not a novelist.

I don't wish to leave the impression that my excursions into the novel were a waste of time. Parts have been salvaged from them: a short story, some memoir pieces and poems. What's more, they put me in touch with a more productive, more consistent way of working: not late at night when the spirit moves, but first thing in the morning and on a regular basis, catching the best energy of the day. In addition, while I was writing fiction I read it intensively, becoming a fan of Chekhov and such contemporary masters as Alice Munro, Don DeLillo and William Trevor. Most important, perhaps, those novels I struggled with and a journal that I kept while working on them helped me extend the range of my material both inwardly toward a core of subjective experience, and outward into the social world.

"By God! I will accept nothing which all cannot have their counterpart of on the same terms."

I stare at Whitman's line and am taken in by it. It seems noble.

Is it? It seems like a more noble attitude than my own selfish, everyday stance: "I want my share, let others look out for themselves."

My view is petty. But what self-assurance this Whitman has. That self-assurance is part of—as Whitman implies—a mystery, a faith.

A while ago, a student of mine was complaining about a certain poet's obscurity. The student was offended at having to look up so many words in hopes of finding the key to poems which finally just didn't 'make it' anyway. Poets, she said, ought not to be obscure—poetry ought to be available to an interested truck driver.

"It is," I said, "through country music." But oh how superior I felt, how condescending as I said it.

Remember the problem I had as a novelist?—that damn audience looking over my shoulder. As a poet, I've been able largely to exclude thoughts of an audience from my study. But there's a price to be paid. Much of what I do is not accessible to everyone. That price seems inevitable in the choice of poetry. Has there ever been a large serious audience for poetry? Large? What scale are we talking about?

Would a few more thousands or even millions of readers make any difference to the quality of what we write? Perhaps a novel can be aimed at a mass audience and not suffer—the novelist has that distance, that objectivity; if not, he or she will be in trouble from the start, as I was. But poetry is the most intimate art and the most subjective.

It has been observed often enough that the audience we have now for poetry is made up largely of the poets themselves. The poets and one or two critics. But is that so bad? By contrast, you often hear the complaint that athletics in the U.S. is made up massively of an audience, which sits on its duff and watches a small group of skilled professionals perform. Wouldn't it be healthier to have a smaller audience and more people participating? And with the recent growth of creative writing programs, poetry does indeed see the audience becoming participants. As Marvin Bell (a runner as well as a poet) has pointed out, it would be foolish to expect that every runner or every poet be of world class caliber, but that's no reason to deny them a chance to run.

It was as an adolescent that I began to read poetry myself, began to take consolation from it, and from the thought that I might one day pull my fragmented self together into that unified creature, The Poet. As you see, I've only been partly successful in this endeavor. But if I have a clear conception of an audience, part of it lies in that adolescent self I once was, whom I try to reach back to. It's he—or that part of him in all of us—that I addressed in the opening lines of my first collection, *The Bone-Duster*:

> Friend, I give you this consolation:
> our losses die with us.

Seen as a whole, the arts are not the work of individuals, but of a community. They are a part of the human effort which can be grouped under the heavy headings, "Culture," and "Civilization." The whole could not possibly be the work of this musician or that painter, of one poet no matter how gifted, or of one sculptor, novelist or choreographer. It is rather an activity which humanity itself seems to participate in. Writing as an individual, I want to maintain my style, my distinctive methods and subjects—in fact I can't help but do this—but I also want to be seen as a part of the larger effort.

I've come quite a distance from my initial subject—but let me push on with this thought. It is wrong to think of the novel as having a mass audience and poetry an audience of just a few. Who is the audience for humanity—for culture as a whole—if not some being outside of culture, outside the world as we know it? This is metaphysics, of course, and takes us to a level of speculation beyond what we can properly articulate.

Rilke was on to this. Perhaps ultimately we write for the angels. And in that case, whether we write novels or poems and whether our audience here is small or vast—these are not the important issues.

ROBERT LOWELL
REMEMBERED

The maples in Harvard Yard were starting to turn and the whole world seemed golden. I'd just checked the bulletin board at Warren House and found my name on his list. Though I'd only read a few of his poems, I knew that Robert Lowell had won a Pulitzer Prize and it seemed to me that being accepted into his writing seminar was equivalent to being admitted into the fellowship of poets. For me, now twenty and a junior, the alternative had gaped large. What if, among aspiring student bards, I'd been spurned as unworthy—plucked up, as it were, and flung from the slopes of Mt. Parnassus into the murky depths where I'd sizzle away to nothing like a chunk of superfluous fat? With relief compounding my joy, my heart rose up and fluttered at the good news.

I don't want to say that Lowell's actual class was a disappointment, but it wasn't what I'd expected. We brought in mimeographed copies of our poems, passed them around and received the rather guarded appraisal of our peers. Lowell himself, handsome, tall, self-conscious and ill-at-ease, would occasionally comment as well, picking out a phrase or a word-choice that struck him as "unusual," which, in the case of my own poems, I took to mean good, though it might just as well have meant the opposite. Sometimes his bony hand would hover over the page as though waiting for a sign, but when the spark came it often launched him on a tangent, bringing to mind a poem by Dickinson, Eliot or Empson that he was more interested in talking about than anything in the half-formed student work before us. Often the class took an odd spin, as if we were there to amuse and stimulate him rather than to be taught. In a sense, he became the subject of the class, since he was showing us how a real poet's mind worked, and that was fine with me.

I observed his gestures—how his index finger would circle thoughtfully, as if stirring a cup of coffee, as he worked through a literary paradox or called up another marvelous poet we *must* read. He introduced the work of his friends and rivals, Elizabeth Bishop, John Berryman, Randall Jarrell, Theodore Roethke, and Philip Larkin, and brought forward older poets who piqued his interest like Yeats, Tennyson, and even, on one occasion, Kipling. He treated the great dead as if they were still alive, mocking any questionable phrasing and pointing out bold images and ingenious structural moves as if they'd been authored by an upstart contemporary he needed to come to grips with. Because he'd noted an oblique connection to my work, I read Berryman's 77 *Dream Songs*, just out, and reviewed it glowingly for the *Advocate*. He also passed around mimeographed copies of some of Sylvia Plath's final poems, since he was writing the introduction to his former student's astonishing collection *Ariel* at the time.

Phil Levine has called Lowell one of the worst teachers he ever had, but I never regretted being in his class, although, in all honesty, I can't say that he taught me much about writing poetry. Even after I'd taken his seminar a second time in my senior year, my style remained a clotted pastiche of phrases that I considered literary and impressive, and when I got to Iowa, the poet George Starbuck held out the sheaf of my undergraduate work as if it gave off a rancid odor, and asked me bluntly: "Why are you writing this stuff?"

Lowell held back his criticism, conscious perhaps of the destructive weight it might carry. Deferring to his students' sensitivities, he let our blunders slide rather than pan a misjudged phrase or malformed stanza and risk snapping a bud off at the stem. Poetry, for him, was not just a craft but a calling or a zone of consciousness and he believed that those of us who might eventually turn into poets would have to learn to make our way alone into that dream-haunted wood.

"My mind's not right," Lowell announces in "Skunk Hour," his famous poem about voyeurism and stubborn survival. We knew that he suffered from manic-depression and when he huddled in a corner of the seminar room, obsessively cleaning his glasses and rambling distractedly about Melville's Captain Ahab as if he knew the man personally, he seemed close to the abyss. For the rest of that semester, William Alfred, his steady friend, a scholar and a successful playwright, filled in. Alfred had a gentle, monkish quality, with a bit of an Irish lilt to his voice and a fringe of graying hair around an egg-shaped dome. He took a more personal interest in his students than Lowell and asked what my plans were following graduation. I said that I wanted to write but had no specific plans. He brought up the Vietnam War and said he'd heard good things about Iowa, pointing out that I'd be able to maintain my student deferment there.

It was at Iowa that I first gave proper attention to Robert Lowell's poetry, which became, and remains, an important influence on my work. Even today, reading *Life Studies*, I can hear his oddly southern drawl (though he came from Boston, of course), picking out choice words and dwelling on favorite phrases, as if he were discovering them for the first time. Unlike his oracular early poems, these have an off-beat, mandarin style, as if bemused with his own madness, his own griefs.

In 1965, Lowell turned down an invitation to the White House and attacked American policy in Vietnam, helping to launch the anti-war movement. Later, on lithium, he would overcome his mania and live out his life as a jet-setter, taking part in several political campaigns and writing prolifically but not nearly as well. I remember my grief tinged with anger when he died, and I recall sitting in a bar in Juneau, Alaska, on a misty November day, accusing him of abusing his talent and of failing to teach me what finally I had needed to teach myself.

SUSPENSION OF DISBELIEF: ON RELIGIOUS POETRY IN A SECULAR AGE

I'm kneeling in church beside our Irish maid, Lilly. This is in New Rochelle, so I must be six. She's holding a string of purple beads, jewel-like pieces of cut glass with some milky white ones spaced out over the string, which I figure are to help her keep count of her prayers. I ask to hold it and try counting the beads. If you do it right, does it make some heavenly force come down through them into your hands? There's a service going on in Latin and as I watch I twist the string and it breaks. The beads come off and I clutch them tightly in my fists. This is awful! I don't want Lilly to know. But eventually she will have to know. I feel I am surely damned and—worse—that she may go to Hell too because of what I've done.

She looks over and sees that I'm crying. I open my hands and show her the beads. She's surprised but then she smiles. It is not as bad as I thought. The beads can be re-strung.

I go around the corner to my friend John Sattler's house on French Ridge. No one is up yet and I've been warned not to ring the doorbell this early, so I sit on the stoop and wait. Bored, I press my hands against the cement steps and examine the pattern of dimples this leaves on my skin.

If it were Sunday, my friend's family would be getting ready for church and I'd be invited in. The Sattlers know that I'm Jewish and are concerned for my soul. Sometimes I go to Mass with them, squeezing into their aging purple Pontiac, and on the way they fill me in about Jesus, Mary and Joseph and various other characters. As a matter of fact, my friend's older brother is named Joseph, and I gather that his mother hopes he'll become a priest. I don't see that he's especially holy yet, but he does seem rather priggish, so maybe that's a start. Like my nursemaid Lilly, the Sattlers figure that when I grow up I'll remember going to Mass with them and decide to become a Catholic. The service is in Latin, but the church has a fine set of stained glass windows and I can stare at the glowing colors and try to figure out the stories they illustrate while the priest drones on.

It's October, 1951, and my folks decide I need to see what temple is like. We aren't religious, so this is in the nature of an educational experience. I learn that the shiny wooden benches are hard for kids to sit on and that the singing of the cantor is sour and melancholy. It seems that these well-off Westchester Jews enjoy hearing about the hard times their Biblical ancestors suffered through. Then the rabbi begins to speak about heroism. He wants to call our attention to a modern-day hero, not an actual Jew, but a true hero in the Biblical tradition nevertheless. It gradually dawns on me that he's speaking of Bobby Thompson, the baseball player whose ninth inning home run recently snatched the pennant from my beloved Brooklyn Dodgers. After the sermon I must shake Rabbi Shankman's hand and say, "Shalom," but there is only bitterness in my heart as I say it.

I want to take as my point of departure some comments on religious art in Jonathan Holden's essay, "Style, Authenticity and Poetic Truth." Holden argues that authenticity in art comes from personally discovered truth and what is made by hand. But he also contends that because religions offer us a "codified system of values—official truth—" they cannot achieve by themselves the kind of hand-made authenticity we find in excellent works of art. "This is why, over and over again, religions resort to the authenticity of art, whether by Tintoretto or Bach, to refurbish their truth. Without the rhetoric of art, such 'truth' would far less efficiently compel...our assent."

While I believe that Holden catches the quality of spontaneously discovered truth which characterizes many of the excellent poems of our time, I don't think his formulation does justice to the religious element in art. When he points to religion's using "the rhetoric of art," that phrase has an edge to it which seems to imply that Bach and Tintoretto were no more than skillful publicists for their respective religions. To the contrary, I suspect the artists themselves would have maintained that their art benefited profoundly from their religious beliefs: consider what a rich context the Gospels provide—how many scenes for the painter, and what impressive texts for the composer.

These days, of course, we need not subscribe to Lutheran doctrine to enjoy Bach's vocal music. Though we may not actually believe it, in listening to the music we "suspend our disbelief." We are for the moment Christianized.

If, as Holden argues, any system of belief is suspect, and truth lies only in what is discovered in the process of making the work of art, I'm afraid the whole art of poetry may be backed into a corner—fated to repeat over and over at a lower level the wonderful but local epiphanies of a James Wright or an Elizabeth Bishop. I want to suggest here an alternative position, for it seems to me that a religion—a systematic tradition of beliefs—can be a very useful thing to have at hand when a poet wants to write something more—or other—than a series of local epiphanies.

I'd never thought seriously about religion since I decided it was all nonsense back in junior high. But a number of years ago, against my rational conviction that the Biblical texts and the miracles on which any logical defense of religion must rest are unworthy of belief, there developed a kind of mental drift toward Christianity. It was I suppose mostly a wish that belief were possible, but a wish so strong that at times I imagined I could accept the whole myth.

What to make of this? I am a scientific rationalist. The big bang, biological evolution, the blank permanence of death—I'm convinced that this kit of irreligious notions adds up to a persuasive hypothesis about our strange and unlikely existence. Yet I was haunted by the other: not the Old Testament stuff, but Christ as dramatized in the Gospel stories and the great Western art which derives from them. Not belief itself, but a ghost of belief offered itself as I lay in bed drowsing, about to fall asleep. And I couldn't decide if I wanted to exorcise the ghost or accept it as real.

It was, I imagine, at least partly a question of self-definition. My identity, otherwise secure, broke apart here, on these ultimate questions. The brain halves, perhaps—rational vs. religious—with the religious half taking over during this pre-sleep state of drowsiness. It was a drama over which I seemed to have little control. Free will? I couldn't even tell how serious the conflict was. By day, I had no problem. But at night, nearing sleep, I could sense a mysterious presence.

Among my earliest memories, I can recall being wheeled to church in a stroller by the Irish maid whose rosary I would later break. No doubt, at three, I was in love with Lilly, and the holy candles she lit, the stained glass she pointed to, her prayers to statues lodged in me at that time. I remember one polished marble sculpture of a small boy sitting in a woman's lap. Lilly told me who they were and explained that the boy, like me, was actually Jewish. Being Jewish was problematic, however, since by explaining Catholicism to me she was exposing me to the perils of apostasy. Now that I knew about the true religion, wouldn't I have to convert or face eternal damnation? She probably figured it was worth the risk, and that my youth would protect me from God's wrath. Back home, though, religion wasn't taken seriously. My family celebrated Passover with a feast and Christmas with a tree, the two rituals more or less canceling each other out.

In the pre-sleep mental image which helped set my 'religious revival' off I seemed to be in a place of large boulders in shadow, but off to one side out of view something was happening in blazing light. I couldn't see what, but felt that it was the Crucifixion. The light in the scene emanated from an off-stage Christ, as in a Rembrandt etching. And it occurred to me at the time that part of the wish for religion was simply my desire for a powerful support on which to rest my poetry.

That's not all, of course. There was also the dread of dying which had become much more real to me with the sudden death of a friend, Gerry Nadel, a journalist and a teacher who was married to my wife's cousin. Gerry was several years younger than I, but one night the outer layer of his heart muscle started to peel off like the skin of an onion. Once started, the process was irreversible, and he died that night on the operating table.

From this period I found myself reading more seriously in religion and philosophy. I had no particular expertise, but having the interest, I felt there ought to be a way to bring this concern into my poetry. I still do not attend church or temple. In fact, my basic beliefs are unchanged. But having learned something about the divided nature of my own consciousness, I hoped to do justice to these religious concerns in my writing.

It seems to me that art allows a poet, a composer, or a painter to adopt a system of beliefs tentatively—as it were *experimentally*—for the purposes of his or her art. The composer—let's say Bach—may choose, though he himself is Protestant, to adopt the Catholic faith in order to compose a mass. How is it possible to affirm a religion which is not your own? Yet Bach does just that in convincing—I would say *authentic* fashion—in his B-Minor Mass. In modern poetry, something similar happens with Yeats's "metaphysics." Did he really believe in those cycles, those historical gyres? The poet himself gives contradictory answers. It seems that in part he did believe—at least for the sake of his poems.

"Suspension of disbelief"—Coleridge's phrase—is usually applied to the audience at a play [1]. The actors must only create a sufficient illusion, and the audience will willingly yield up the knowledge that the players on stage are not really the people they pretend to be. For my purposes, though, I'm applying the phrase not to the audience but to the artist, the poet. In a secular time, it seems to me permissible for the poet to suspend her or his disbelief in religion in order to find out where it can lead the poem.

[1] The phrase occurs in Chapter XIV of *Biographia Literaria,* but see also Coleridge's treatment of dramatic illusion in his lecture on *The Tempest.*

Let me give a personal example. I've always wanted to write poems on a larger scale than the one or two page lyric, and, to make further difficulties for myself, I wanted those longer poems to be philosophical rather than narrative in organization. Eliot's *Four Quartets* provided one of the models I had in mind, but I wondered, having no deep religious beliefs, how I should proceed.

I didn't know, had no real theory; but one day a number of years ago I began to accumulate lines and stanzas that seemed to be grouping themselves into such a poem. The poem's central consciousness—not me exactly, but some version of me—was engaged in trying to reconcile two different kinds of thinking—one Medieval, the other modern. I'd read myself into the Medieval period through several books on Kabbalah, a form of Jewish mysticism, by the historian Gershom Scholem[2].

Only in a highly metaphorical sense—if at all—could any of what these mystics said be affirmed by a modern sensibility. The Kabbalists believed, for example, that the letters of the Hebrew alphabet were mystical symbols, and that words and sentences in the Bible could be reinterpreted to give meanings not at all apparent in the surface narratives.

Kabbalists wrote about an initial *breaking of the vessels* meant to contain God's light—a great flaw in the universe prior even to Adam's fall. As the light scattered, the power of evil was released. Only then was Adam created in order to remedy the situation. He failed, and as a consequence, we are all in exile, our task to gather up the dispersed sparks of light through religious acts. Exile becomes a mission and when our job is done comes the Messiah. Beyond this metaphysic, there is also a great deal of magic and superstition—demons, incantations—connected with Kabbalism, as well as a rich tradition of metaphor and myth.

At the same time that I was reading this material, I was also looking into Ernst Cassirer's *Language and Myth* and Nietzsche's fiercely skeptical *Twilight of the Idols*. It wasn't a religious conversion that I was seeking, but rather a means of organizing and expressing the tensions between skepticism and belief.

---

[2] *Major Trends in Jewish Mysticism* and *On the Kaballah and Its Symbolism.*

Few readers of "The Cyclist," the poem that resulted, will pick up on the Kabbalistic element. The doctrines are just too far from common experience, and I try to introduce them in language which allows them to be taken simply as metaphor—which in a sense they are. But what most readers should see in this poem is a kind of spiritual quest. Here are the opening stanzas:

> A chill summer day, the sky
> a varied gray with squalls to the north
> and west, as I pedal shifting gears,
> watching for glass. A swallow-tail
> flirts for a second with the eye,
> a runner passes, bare-chested
> in green shorts. And in the bushes
>
> beside the road as my bicycle coasts,
> the smell of rotting flesh. Objects
> and our ideas about the word
> grow and decay. One
> month from forty; to my right the river
> slides its scaly back. "The world
> is flat"—such facts for text,
>
> grasped trembling like that aspen
> leaf, twisting on a point I can't
> connect: as I move among
> gusty ghosts, however fast,
> I am this single place,
> a man on a bike—he goes
> and the world stays...

Throughout the writing of the poem, I was aware that its subject required a special tact in order to avoid offence, not just to the religious sensibility, but to my own skepticism as well. Three quarters of what I wrote for it had ultimately to be scrapped. And even as it stands, now finished, the poem is perhaps only a pointer toward future poems which may be more successful in incorporating similar themes. But in "The Cyclist" for practically the first time, I allowed myself to use religious terms, to speak of prayer and "the soul," and to speculate on the deeds and wishes of God.

In his essay which sparked some of these thoughts, Jonathan Holden opposes poetic truth to the truth of religious doctrines on the one hand and that of modern science on the other. Poetry's truth is concerned with values and that of science with facts, but what about religion? It seems to me that religion is concerned with both values and facts, though we have come to regard many of the "facts" of religion as myth rather than, say, history or cosmology.

Religion is not, as Holden would have it, merely a codified series of "thou shalts"; rather it is a way of thinking about myth. Religions, in effect, bring order to myth and superstition; they structure those primitive tales and beliefs that come out of our deepest questioning. Even today religious thought can open up the stage of the individual consciousness, and put us in touch with another part of what it means to be human.

But I don't want to underestimate the problems in making use of religious materials. For most of us, as Wallace Stevens says, the gods have been "dispelled in mid-air." I am not more patient than the next reader with the sort of poem that dusts off the Greek pantheon and brings it forward like so much cultural bric-a-brac. Nor is Milton's stated project of justifying the ways of God to man easily available today.

Without traditional belief, then, if I want to write poems that reach toward ultimate things, it may be necessary to put aside my disbelief. I enter this world in a spirit of exploration, surrounded by mists and mysteries. I have only a little craft, which I must steer with caution and with whatever wit I can muster.

II.

BECOMING A POET

FIRSTLINGS

After readings, when I take questions from the audience, I'm likely to be asked how I became a poet in the first place. It seems like such a wildly impractical choice, and yet somehow appealing as well. I tell them that in my case (as, I suspect, with many other poets) it goes back to junior high. Like many kids, I'd spent most of my childhood fascinated with fossils, and when asked what I planned to be when I grew up, second on my list (once I'd retired from playing first-base for the Brooklyn Dodgers) came the more plausible goal of being a fossil hunter. Poetry was not on my radar.

By eighth grade, however, my sweet boy-soprano had given way to a croaking baritone and I dropped out of choir. I went on several dates, but these were far from satisfactory, since my motives were suspect and the girls were chiefly concerned with showing off their fancy dresses. My main extra-curricular activity was the science club. And then somehow, amid the push and pull of hormonal mood swings and identity issues, I discovered poetry.

For an English assignment in ninth grade, I memorized and recited "Fern Hill." We had the recording at home and I tried to imitate Dylan Thomas's stirring delivery. Then when my mother took me to a bookstore to pick out a birthday present for myself, I surprised us both by choosing a fat Louis Untermeyer anthology of British and American poetry. I worked my way forward from Chaucer through Shakespeare, Keats, the two Brownings, Dickinson, and Eliot, before settling for a while on Algernon Charles Swinburne for his hypnotic rhythms, gaudy alliteration and morbid sentiments.

The first poem I ever wrote spilled over from this reading and from my muddled emotional life. It described a wild team of galloping horses—not a subject I knew much about first hand, but of course the point was symbolic. The apocalyptic horses were compared to a racing heart and stood in my mind for death and for sexual passion, and the rhythm tried to imitate their thunderous headlong rush. Putting it through several revisions allowed me to relive the experience of creating the poem in the first place and the whole process gave me something to do with my turbulent feelings, which otherwise threatened to run away with me like those galloping horses.

I felt encouraged enough by the results to try again a few months later. My second poem was about a star. It had regular rhyming stanzas and used the obscure poetic word "dartle" to describe the distant stellar object, which stood for the girl—was it Susan or Stephanie?—I was secretly in love with at the moment. I took the project seriously enough to fill several notebook pages with alternative versions. It was, to my mind, a more sophisticated effort than the wild horse poem though perhaps not as spontaneous. I hoped to create a crafted object external to myself, something that might be of interest to other readers of the Untermeyer anthology.

My interest in fossils continued on a separate track, and toward the end of tenth grade my father wrote to Yale's Peabody Museum, asking if I could work there as a summer volunteer. For the next two summers I commuted in relative comfort from our suburban New York home to New Haven, against the dense flow of fathers going the other way. I remember my first morning on the job, when Professor Gregory, after pointing out some highlights of the public exhibit, stepped around a barrier in the museum's elegant gray-stone lobby and led me downstairs to the basement, where thousands of ancient bones were stored in drawers lined up floor to ceiling in three large galleries. He handed me a small vacuum cleaner, a dust mop and brush, and explained my task. Using a step ladder to reach the upper drawers, I was to work in these poorly lit stacks, removing decades of dust and grime from the thirty million year-old bones in the museum's extensive oreodont collection.

Bones are shocking things—loveliness and horror juxtaposed. Their curves, knobs and hollows attract the eye like sculpture, but this scaffolding only emerges after flesh and sinew have rotted away. Then a tiny proportion of them, darkened and mineralized, transformed in both color and substance, may by luck and natural processes overcome the universal catastrophe of time. Those that survive provide us with a keyhole into a legendary prehistoric world.

Though I'd hoped to do something more exciting than dusting them, this job still beat my other option—tabulating surveys for my father's market research firm—and I stuck it out for two summers, partly because all fossils, even the apparently insignificant remains of oreodonts, like those saintly femurs and knuckle-bones preserved in jeweled boxes in the crypts of Italian churches, retained an aspect of the sacred for me. The ritual of cleaning them engaged my spiritual side in a way that my father's surveys about soft drinks and toothpastes never could and, in addition, I figured—correctly as it turned out—that the work would serve as an apprenticeship, opening up the more challenging world of exploration and discovery for me later on.

"But why oreodonts?" you may ask. And I did ask, though not out loud. Oreodonts were fossil pig-like creatures that had once flourished in large herds in the western United States but went extinct long before humans came on the scene. My real interest was in dinosaurs of course, but by the logic of science, at least in biology, you can start almost anywhere and by comparing specimens learn to distinguish one species from its cousins by noting, in the case of oreodonts for example, the number and size of the teeth and the arrangement of cusps on particular molars. When you master one group, you can move on to a related form, and then another, in an ever widening circle of knowledge.

Interestingly, in *The ABC of Reading* Ezra Pound cites this approach to scientific investigation as the correct way to go at poetry as well. "The proper METHOD for studying poetry and good letters is the method of contemporary biologists, that is careful first-hand examination of the matter, and continual COMPARISON of one 'slide' or specimen with another."

Professor Gregory must have assumed that I would pick up the salient features that distinguished the various types of oreodonts as I advanced with brush, mop and vacuum from drawer to dusty drawer, and in a rudimentary way I suppose I did, although the details are long gone from me now.

I bagged my lunch, a bologna sandwich and chips, and ate it upstairs in the Ornithology wing, which in contrast to the musty basement was air-conditioned and lit by dozens of fluorescent bulbs. The specimens here were also kept in drawers, but instead of bones these held the feathered skins of thousands of sparrows and more exotic species, which the ornithologists had shot on field trips to such places as Peru and New Guinea. It puzzled me that they would kill those beautiful creatures in order to study them, but of course obsessions are not incompatible with murder, and the scientists seemed perfectly comfortable with their professional conduct as they chatted expertly about the make and caliber of rifle they'd used to poach an especially prized specimen.

The ornithologists were social creatures and welcomed my visits even though I wasn't strictly a member of their clan. On one occasion, I recall, the eminent birder Roger Tory Peterson dropped by. He had popping eyes and a beak-like nose, and he moved his head in a nervous, pecking sort of way. He was treated with great deference during the visit but after he left everyone cackled over his avian looks and manner.

Later on, my museum work would pay off in an unexpected way, when I opened the drawers of memory and unpacked that redolent world in the title poem of my first collection, "The Bone-Duster":

> Two adolescent summers
> wasting in the basement
> of the Peabody Museum
> the dampness from stones
> rising along my arms, sleeveless as I dusted
> the bones of
> a thousand extinct pigs: it seems
> I have written about this before,
> moving down the stacks from drawer
>
> to drawer, seems I
> will always be writing the poems
> that might have soothed me
> then. Then as now
> the smell of damp stones, of
> bones, of wood aging, in basements and slow dust,
> pieces of tedium drifting down
> and down on the calm air.

And then up to lunch
    in the bright fluorescent
hall of birds, table on
table lined with limp bodies, sparrows and weavers,
auks, hawks, and puffins, all typed, all
labeled, gold-, red-, green-, and brown-feathered lumps
laid out behind us as we ate.

                Again
I toss my lunch bag
into the bin, again the slow freight
elevator, dim and rusting,
lowers me down and down.

A warm summer night. Too young to drive, I wander restlessly through our neighborhood on foot. Tall trees—oaks, maples, elms—line the streets. Some of the largest houses have white columned porticos and extensive lawns, though my own block, with facing three-story homes and a couple of smaller ranch houses including ours, is far more modest. Under the stars at Beechmont Lake, I clutch a slim black-bordered paperback and read by a street lamp's amber light:

I saw the best minds of my generation destroyed by madness,
    starving hysterical naked,
dragging themselves through the negro streets at dawn looking for
    an angry fix,
angelheaded hipsters burning for the ancient heavenly connection to the
    starry dynamo in the machinery of night...

As I chant Allen Ginsberg's passionate litany of desire and complaint, I feel that his manic frenzy perfectly matches my own.

    At a time when conformity ruled, "Howl" demonstrated that there was another way. By my senior year in high school I had taken this outsider role to heart. Flaunting my eccentricities—a writer of poetry, a lover of classical music, a would-be fossil hunter—did I actually wear a beret? For a while I think I did.

Over my parent's objections, I let my hair grow and unknown to them carried a nasal spray bottle filled with vodka to spike my orange juice at lunch. On one occasion, I overdid it and nodded off in chemistry class, almost toppling out of my seat. Mr. Wagner got a big kick out of that and never let me live it down.

Throughout high school I continued to read and write poetry. It was not an activity that my teachers supported or even knew about. It was something I did on the side when I should have been working on trigonometry or memorizing dates. I wrote a sequence of love sonnets, modeled, I thought, on Shakespeare, and more successfully several scattered free verse experiments derived from e.e. cummings. One jazz-loving friend, took an interest in my writing, but no one else. But though I wrote in seclusion, I was not without ambition, figuring that someday my work would surely get the recognition it deserved.

My motives for writing haven't changed that much over the years. Poems still help me work through my mental morass and reach out to others with a crafted presentation of my thoughts, emotions and dreams, hoping for a response. The poems themselves improved as I developed a better ear for tone and got a handle on some of the formal elements of verse, but the essentials were there from the start, in particular a willingness to look over what I'd scribbled in a moment of frenzy and try to make it stronger both aesthetically and as a piece of communication. And behind this strange activity, I was, it seems, trying to revise and perfect my mixed-up adolescent self.

THE DIG AT POLECAT BENCH: SUMMER, 1961

Prof. Glenn L. Jepsen, trim, graying, older than I'd expected, led me down to the basement of the museum at Princeton and pulled out an intricate golf ball-size skull from one of the Paleocene drawers. Using a pocket magnifying glass, he showed me the structure of tiny bones around the ear but his explanation quickly outpaced my grasp of cranial anatomy.

"We'll be looking for more of these," he said dryly.

Then, after reviewing my background—the early fascination with dinosaurs and my volunteer work at Yale's Peabody Museum—Jepsen asked me whether I thought I could hold up over ten weeks of digging out in the Wyoming badlands. "It goes well up over 100 degrees out there," he warned, "and there's no shade to speak of."

I brought up my camping trip to the Southwest a few summers before and told him the heat hadn't bothered me. As an aside I conceded that toward the end of that trip I'd fallen off a cliff.

"*Really?* Any broken bones?"

"Just my skull."

I'd hoped to pass this off as a joke, but Jepsen held up a hand for me to stand still, took my chin between thumb and forefinger and directed it to the side. He was a careful observer, and as he continued to check me out, noting the crook in my nose, my blue-gray eyes and teenage acne, I wondered if he thought he could penetrate my character by scrutinizing the contours of my skull.

It was only a tiny fracture, I explained, and had never shown up on the x-rays. True, I'd been unconscious for three days, but I was okay now, I insisted, adding that I really wanted to come on the expedition.

Apparently satisfied, Jepsen said that he had reservations about my youth but since he was short of hands and I had a strong recommendation from Dr. Gregory of Yale, he was willing to take me along. Then, as we moved toward the staircase, he asked: "By the way, Mr. Morgan, what is your family's religion?"

The anti-Semitism at Princeton was no secret. The *Times* had run articles about discrimination at the eating clubs there. But I found it hard to believe that a scientist like Jepsen would have anything to do with it. Didn't science require an objective, facts-based point of view?

"We're not religious," I said after a pause.

"That's not what I meant—as you well know!" His face reddened. "You aren't by any chance Jewish, are you?" His anger startled me, although it's true I had tried to duck his question. He obviously wasn't having any of that.

While being Jewish had little to do with who I thought I was—we celebrated Christmas rather than Hanukah and I'd only attended one Friday night service, nearly ten years before—still, my family was Jewish in the racial sense that Jepsen had in mind.

When I conceded as much, the professor turned and walked away. We were in a dim-lit corner of the basement near the staircase and an image of an SS officer interrogating a wartime prisoner flickered briefly in my mind. But this was America, not Nazi Germany. How could it be happening here?

Jepsen returned and, facing me again, said coldly that he would have to rethink our arrangement. I asked what he meant.

"I'm sorry, Mr. Morgan, but under the circumstances I'm afraid you won't be able to come on the expedition after all."

"But I thought we'd agreed!"

Jepsen shrugged. It was as if we had entered a different geological era, a new ice-age perhaps, in which prior categories no longer applied.

Stunned, holding back tears, I asked how I was supposed to explain this to my folks.

He waved his hand dismissively. "Tell them whatever you like."

But I wasn't ready to give up. "Well, what about Prof. Gregory?"

Jepsen stared at me. In the small world of vertebrate paleontology, he and the Yale professor were colleagues, publishing in the same journals and attending professional meetings together.

Of course he could always say that he'd turned me down because I was too young but I would have a different explanation, and Jepsen must have sensed that his anti-Semitic views might not fly with the other scientist.

There could have been other factors as well. I sensed he was taken aback by my youthful vehemence and he may even have been moved by my distress. But, whatever the reason, after some reflection he reversed himself and allowed that I could come on the expedition after all.

On the train ride home from Princeton, after scanning the racy cartoons and the naked centerfold in the magazine I'd picked up earlier in the day, I plunged into a wordy discourse on 'the *Playboy* philosophy.' I had to agree with the writer that Puritanism was long out of date; the problem was that none of the girls I knew seemed to realize this yet.

Then I had an encouraging thought. It struck me that Professor Jepsen probably hadn't run into many Jews at Princeton, and so his prejudice might just reflect the stereotypes circulating in that narrow community. Faced with new evidence, he would naturally, as a man of science, want to correct any errors in his thinking. So by holding up under the sizzling badlands sun and displaying my sterling character over the course of the summer, I figured I could set him straight.

Of course I should have talked matters over with my folks. But, knowing that they might well refuse to let me go, I said nothing. My only alternative for the summer involved the dreary task of tabulating questionnaires at my father's market research firm in the city, while the expedition definitely appealed to my adventurous side. Up to now I'd been telling people that I planned to be a professional paleontologist and here was my chance to find out what that really meant. Besides, whatever the outcome, I told myself that it would all be over in a couple of months, after which I was heading off to a brand new life as a Harvard freshman.

I flew by jet to Minneapolis, then switched to a twin-engine prop-plane that hopped across North Dakota to a town called

Dickinson in the southwest corner of the state. Miss North Dakota happened to be on the plane too and the star-struck flight attendants insisted that she should get off first and have the ladder to herself. The rest of us waited at our seats as she freshened her rouge and lipstick, and made sure her wavy blond hair was just so. Then, like a miraculous creature from another world, she descended to the dusty tarmac where a delegation of city fathers had gathered to greet her. One of them hurried forward with a parasol to shield her from the blazing sun.

Annoyed with the delay this small-town ritual had caused to his schedule, Jepsen led me to his aging Ford pick-up and we drove out to the dig-site.

Almost fifty years later, how much of the present account can I vouch for? In the intervening time, my memories of that summer, with a good deal of heightening and fabrication, have been transferred to fiction and poetry, and sometimes it's hard to tell which of the images in my mind were invented, which real. Googling for assistance, however, I came up with a photograph of Glenn Lowell Jepsen on the web, along with a glowing account of his career.

Much younger than when I knew him, he wears a trim goatee and an open collared shirt in the photo, with a small tobacco pouch and a couple of pens in the left-hand pocket. The goatee and pouch ring a bell—yes, I remember them—but the jaunty grin he flashes at the camera—a hint of Indiana Jones glinting from his eyes—suggests an aspect of his character that had eroded away by the time I knew him. From the text, I learn that he was born in Lead, South Dakota and grew up in Rapid City, and I find this quote attributed to him: "Expeditions to collect long-dead bones and other fossils have been significant not only in obtaining valuable specimens but also in the more important sphere of influencing men's lives."

The biography also includes a description of his approach to fossil hunting: "Jepsen's patient and persistent collecting of the Paleocene fauna of Polecat Bench in Wyoming resulted in Princeton's possessing one of the best collections of this type in North America.... [He] endeavored to understand as completely as possible the animals and environment that existed during one of the most crucial epochs in mammalian evolution."

Reassured by how closely this account jibes with my recollections of our enterprise, I call up my disappointment that we wouldn't be devoting any time on the massive dinosaur bones—the ribs and plates of a stegosaurus—that could be seen eroding out of a nearby formation. Unlike the famous expeditions that Roy Chapman Andrews led into the Gobi Desert in search of monsters and marvels a generation earlier, our trip was focused on the meticulous gathering of small, often fragmentary specimens intended to throw light on one local ecosystem—the swampy estuary which had covered that part of Wyoming about sixty-five million years ago. It was a project that Jepsen had already been working on for several years and so our chances of coming up with anything strikingly new were not great. But he wasn't looking to stock his museum's display cases. Instead, our findings would be folded into a statistical survey of the regional fauna, a project that Jepsen (as opposed to the old time fossil hunters, who aspired to fame and gaudy headlines) considered "real science."

The group included two Dartmouth students with their affable professor, a geologist known to everyone as "the Boss," and Pete Robinson, a Yale post-doc whom I knew from my summers at the Peabody. There was also one Princeton graduate student along, but it didn't occur to me, at least at first, to wonder why Jepsen had attracted such a small following from his own institution. Later, we would be joined by a gregarious biker from Rensselaer Polytech.

After a few days walking the floor of an ancient seabed near Dickinson with little to show, we packed our gear into a couple of trucks and moved on to the main locality near Powell in north-central Wyoming. We set ourselves up on the ground floor of an abandoned farmhouse, laying our sleeping bags on top of bare mattresses and sleeping three to a room. An old refrigerator rattled and hummed and to flush the toilet you had to fill a metal bucket at the tub and pour it into the open tank. Jepsen had rented himself more comfortable lodgings in another farmhouse a few miles down the road.

"Up, Morgan, up!" The Boss stood over me, bare-chested, waving a glass of water.

"Let him have it," said Ned Dickey. Hands on hips, the skinny Dartmouth undergraduate grinned down.

The Boss tilted the glass and a splat of water hit me on the forehead. I scrambled to a sitting position, wiping my head with a forearm.

"Hey, give him the whole glass!" said Steve. A big blond with a crew-cut, he stood behind the other two bouncing up and down like a fan at a boxing match. "No mercy, Boss. Don't coddle the shirker!"

"Hey, I'm up! I'm up!"

"The gong sounded seven minutes ago." The Dartmouth professor drew the glass back slowly and swung it forward. Lifting both arms in surrender, I saw the waterline hold at the lip.

"Okay," said the Boss. He wore sneakers, khaki shorts and wire-rimmed glasses. Hummocky tufts of hair, gray mixed with black, receded from his tan forehead. "He's finally cracking."

Six days a week, we drove out to the badlands on the eastern edge of Polecat Bench, where, on top of a small butte, we worked with a dentist's assortment of chisels and picks, uncovering the bones and teeth of the frogs, lizards and early mammals that had lived here during the Paleocene. Like a voyage back through time, the forty minute drive from our decaying farmhouse out to the dig site still holds its drama for me.

With the low sun booming in our faces, we raced through irrigated farm country, then turned north and climbed a set of steep switchbacks to the top of Polecat Bench. We listened to the seven o'clock news as we drove, often hearing Paul Harvey pour his reactionary bilge over the country's young Catholic president, then in his first year of office. Jepsen would urge us to "keep it down" while Harvey's caustic Midwest accent inflamed the airwaves.

The bench itself, a flat prairie with grasses and sagebrush, a few scattered bushes and no trees, was fenced for cattle but we rarely saw any and it must have appeared much as it had decades or even centuries before. Turning off the paved road, we followed an old set of ruts to the edge of the bench, then forsook even that trail, clambering over rocks and dipping into gullies, while the tools in the metal bed behind us rattled and screeched. Creeping along the eastern edge where the prairie eroded into badlands, we could see oil wells punching into the crust of the earth in the barren country down below, while the jagged Bighorn Mountains framed the horizon a hundred miles off. We pulled up at the base of the small butte where the formation that interested Jepsen lay on top near the surface.

Each day we climbed the butte, cleared off a section of the overlying conglomerate, and settled ourselves down to peel away the wafer-thin layers of shale which contained—but not in any great quantity—the fossils we were looking for. Whole mornings might go by with only one or two finds. Against this blue-gray rock the tiny bones and teeth were brown and extremely fragile. When something of interest turned up, Jepsen and the other senior paleontologists would pull out their magnifying glasses, consult, and then inform us that the fossil appeared to be the molar of an early lemur or perhaps the limb-bone of an insectivore. Once, I recall, a string of four or five beautifully articulated vertebrae were judged to be the remains of an ancient garter snake. Leaving the fossils embedded in the rock, the professors would paint them with shellac and set them aside to harden. Then, wrapped in newspaper, they were sent back east for careful extraction and study in the lab.

I soon found that by taking off my glasses I could work closer to the shale whose wave-like patterns of striations etched themselves into my consciousness. It was a little like prying sheets of mica apart, although the shale was more rigid than mica and fractured more easily.

On a lunch break—the usual peanut butter and Kool-Aid—I noticed a burnt match stick on the ground. Strange, since I hadn't seen anyone smoking. But when I nudged it with my boot, it buzzed up into my face. I tried to slap it away but the wasp looped back around and stung me on the palm.

"Let's see it." Jepsen thrust out a hand.

He took my wrist, searching for a pulse. Then, staring into my face, he poked at the small red bump.

"Not numb then. Can you make a fist?" Jepsen pursed his lips and, my anger flaring, I recalled how my friend Flip Cowan would sputter and lean way back, fist cocked, as he delivered Jackie Gleason's line about socking you...*Pow, right in the kisser!*

Still not satisfied, Jepsen ordered me to sit by myself for a while.

"I'm okay," I told him. "I feel fine."

But he insisted. Was I being punished for getting stung? With nothing to do, I twiddled my thumbs and watched the oil wells down below slowly spin their wheels. Then I went over in my head the two or three girls I'd kissed in the past year, the two I'd fooled around with after a graduation party, and the one I loved unabashedly but couldn't get to first base with.

When Jepsen checked back thirty minutes later, he seemed relieved. "Well, at least you're not having an allergic reaction, Mr. Morgan. Good thing—it's a long way to the nearest hospital."

The confusing tangle of emotions that I felt toward Jepsen and that he apparently felt toward me, didn't carry over to the rest of the crew. Nobody else on the expedition cared that I was Jewish, and though at first I felt isolated because of my age, that problem eased once I'd made friends with the two Dartmouth students. Bright but not very intellectual, Ned, a preppy on the varsity ski team, and Steve, a big blonde shot-putter, were not all that different from the jocks I knew back home. During breaks, Steve worked on his form by hurling shot-sized chunks of stone off the butte and we'd watched them arc out and kick up small explosions of dirt as they clattered down the steep slope into the badlands below.

When I mentioned that I'd run track in high school and added—exaggerating my limited ice-time—that I'd played some hockey too, they took me on as a promising recruit, offering me their raunchy slant on college life. My ears burned with their foul-mouthed banter about loose chippies, boozy frat parties, and bawdy road trips, as well as the blow-by-blow accounts they gave of their astonishing sexual exploits. I began to wonder if Harvard would turn out to be the kind of sheltered intellectual experience I'd been anticipating. Steve was headed for the Peace Corps after college, he said, while Ned planned to pursue a career in petroleum geology, because, as he noted, "That's where the big bucks are."

Sometime during the second week, Pete Robinson pulled me aside. We sat on the ground in a shaded area near the edge of the bench and he picked up a small rock and inspected it, rolling it around in his hands. A big friendly guy with a round moon of a face, he seemed strangely ill at ease.

"So how are things going for you, John?" He tossed the rock away. I said fine.

"Well," he said, "something's come up. Professor Jepsen asked me to speak to you. He's worried that we aren't making enough progress out here. He says we're not finding enough stuff to justify the cost."

"But that's not my fault, is it?"

"He doesn't think you're working hard enough."

"I'm doing the same as everybody else."

"He says you have a tendency to daydream. And the other day, sweeping out the farmhouse, he feels you weren't pulling your weight."

"But that's crazy! Most of the time he wasn't even there."

Pete motioned for me to keep my voice down. "I guess he got it from the Boss." He looked across to the mountains. "I'm afraid there's more to it. He's thinking of sending you home. He says you're too young for this work."

I was staggered. Less than a quarter of the way into the expedition, and already I'd been judged a failure. How would I explain this back home—to my friends, to my folks? "But how is he going to find more stuff with fewer people working?"

"If you really want to stay, I can talk to him. But you should think about whether that's the smart thing to do…I mean, under the circumstances."

His last phrase finally tipped me off. "So it's not because I'm too young, right? It's because I'm too Jewish."

"Have you ever run into that kind of thing before?"

I shook my head. "I just don't see what that has to do with anything!"

Pete seemed a little taken aback but I insisted I wanted to stay. Given more time, I still hoped to win Jepsen over.

"Well, okay. I'll tell him that we talked and that you've promised to put out more of an effort. You'll do that, won't you?"

I nodded.

"But be aware that you'll to have to do more than everyone else to satisfy him."

So many years later, it's difficult for me to refute the charge that I was a goof-off. Faced with our tedious day-long scraping away at the rocks, my commitment to fossil hunting had started to waver. Instead of opening up a new chapter in the history of life on earth, it seemed to me that we were merely jotting a few notes in the margins of a well-established text. And I was coming to understand that this was the kind of work that most scientists do most of the time. Making major discoveries is a matter of rare luck. It can't be counted on and in the meantime you have to keep busy and focus your efforts on achievable goals, goals that will lead to publishable results.

Ironically, it seems likely that just a foot or two down from where we were digging lay traces of the massive comet that had put a convulsive end to the Age of Dinosaurs. But that revolutionary idea wouldn't emerge for another decade, and in any case the target audience for our summer's labors was not the general public, eager for fiery cataclysms, but rather a handful of specialists with an interest in the obscure faunas of the Paleocene.

If it sounds like I was becoming cynical about my summer job, in another sense cynicism was what I was fighting against. Full of hidden ambition, I rebelled against the tepid reality of our dig. And at the same time, I was being pulled toward another career, one which I'd begun to explore during high school—becoming a writer. In addition to Darwin's *Voyage of the Beagle*, I'd brought a translation of Dante's *Inferno* along, as well as novels by Henry James and William Golding, and a paperback anthology of contemporary poetry. With no TV in the farmhouse, I had plenty of time to read and to scribble my youthful verses into a spiral notebook.

In addition to stirring up misgivings about my future in paleontology, Jepsen's behavior raised another issue. Though my father's business partner had lost both his parents to the Nazis, none of our close relatives had died in the Holocaust. But now for the first time, I realized that in a crunch I could not escape my Jewish inheritance. Despite my thorough assimilation, my blue eyes and Anglicized name, in any similar crisis I would be pegged as a Jew by the Jepsens of the world. And so, for the first time, I began to wonder just what my Jewish heritage consisted of.

Other than the Passover seders we celebrated with my father's relatives, I'd had little connection with formal Judaism. Both my parents had put religion behind them and, generalizing from too small a sample—the kids I knew well—I assumed that religion was on its way out. But of course that's not what being Jewish meant to Jepsen. As a scientist and a Darwinian, it wasn't a question of beliefs for him but of something you carried in your blood, in your genes.

Although I didn't realize it at the time, the concept of Nordic racial superiority has a long intellectual history in this country. The famous paleontologist Henry Fairfield Osborn, a Princeton man himself and later head of the American Museum of Natural History, wrote the preface to *The Passing of the Great Race* by Madison Grant, in which Grant argued in favor of blocking the immigration of members of inferior groups—mainly Jews, Negroes, and southern Europeans—because they would inevitably contaminate the gene pool. Already, Grant claimed, "the whole tone of American life, social, moral and political has been lowered and vulgarized by them." Both Osborn and Grant were leaders in the eugenics movement of the Twenties and Thirties, and their arguments for racial purity may well have influenced Nazi thinking on the subject. And more than likely they'd influenced Jepsen's thinking too.

As I tried to work my way into the professor's point of view, it struck me that something visceral and compelling must be at stake to make a rational man like Jepsen go so far off track. Was it conceivable that his prejudice had led him to blame me for the expedition's overall bad luck—as if my Jewishness were being rebuked by the very stones we chiseled on? It seemed bizarre, since back home, I was often mistaken for a gentile. But as the facts of my identity became distorted in the lens of air between us, its skewed reflection made me question who I was. Could it be that my words and gestures, in so far as they pointed to my ethnic background, unavoidably offended him? Did I give off a nasty odor undetectable to me, or, like a scorpion, was I blind to my own repulsive nature?

But it was not so much that Jepsen didn't like me, as that he didn't like someone who, I felt, *wasn't* me. I'd never considered being a Jew an important aspect of my identity, but my Jewishness was mainly what he saw. If he'd simply been a fool or a pompous ass, I could have shrugged it off, but he wasn't that. When he turned in a slow circle and pointed out the many ancient geological formations visible from our butte, or when, from a single BB-sized tooth, he pinpointed the prehistoric creature it came from, I had to respect his expertise. He was in a sense, what I'd hoped to become, a successful paleontologist and a distinguished professor. I'd even imagined him—though this hope was rapidly fading—as an important mentor for me.

For the time being, Jepsen let me stay, but he kept his eye on me and when I started to grow a beard quickly put his foot down. It was too scraggly, he said, and made me look like a beatnik. We were here representing two distinguished institutions and needed to be mindful of our appearance. But the skeptic in me wondered who, in this remote cow country, we were trying to impress. Granted, the beard would take a little time to fill in, but I had to question if his real complaint wasn't that it made me look more Jewish.

I held out for a few days before bowing to his wishes and shaving it off. But then an odd thing happened. Jepsen inspected my face and expressed concern that the razor had aggravated my acne. He asked if that was why I'd grown the beard in the first place and apologized for making me shave it off. Had he begun to mellow toward me? Maybe things would work out between us after all.

A few days later out at the butte, I flipped over a sliver of shale and uncovered a significant fossil. Not a complete skull like the one he'd shown me in the museum, but a full upper jaw with most of the teeth in place. Finally some excitement! Jepsen tagged it as a new species, a specimen he could certainly write up for one of the journals.

It was just the luck of the draw that I'd happened to find this nifty fossil, but to my surprise that wasn't how the others looked at it. To them it was as if I'd hit a game-winning triple that could signal the end of our summer-long slump. The next day Jepsen called me aside and offered to write a note of introduction to his friend George Gaylord Simpson, the distinguished Harvard paleontologist. Assuming I went on with fossil hunting, I'd be studying with Simpson in college.

"You are planning to go on?" Jepsen asked.

I told him I thought so, but that I hadn't made a final decision yet.

As soon as the summer was over I began to write about it. My first semester in college, I drafted twenty pages of a stream-of-consciousness novel (we were reading swatches of Joyce's *Ulysses* in a freshman lit class) but nothing more came of this. Later, in graduate school at Iowa, I plunged in again and wrote several chapters which drew a mixed response. My poetry instructor, George Starbuck, was enthusiastic, but when I showed the draft to Kurt Vonnegut he complained that I'd given way too much space to my central character's inner muddle and not enough to presenting the reader with some clear dramatic action. Ten years later, taking Vonnegut's criticism to heart, I started over and managed to complete the book. An agent liked it well enough to shop it around but it had no takers. It seemed as if I were trying to catch a shifty cricket in my hands and every time I grasped for it, it darted away.

But that summer remains active in me. Occasionally I dream about it and at times I can transport myself back.

Needing to take a piss, I step from the cab of the pick-up onto the open bench-land. As I unzip, I glance up at the vast cloud-speckled sky spreading toward the mountains. A shiver between my shoulder blades and a quickening pulse suddenly make me aware of the distance that I've come. How inconceivable this magnificent sweep of prairie would be to my friends back home in the suburbs! And I sense that this openness has a spiritual component, an underlying order not based on the mechanics of the clock or on straight lines and left or right-hand turns, but on the fractal patterns of meandering streams, the mysterious uplift of mountains and the immensity of space and time. It's as if a new dimension has invaded me, opening up niches that I didn't know were there. The smell of sage, the red dirt, the breeze riffling through low grasses, the mountains, the huge sky all seem to carry some message, hard to grasp but deep and lasting, as if I've been given entry to the vastness of the geologic time.

Jepsen leans on the horn. "Come on, Mr. Morgan." Frowning, he sticks his head out the window. "We don't have all day!"

Our five-and-a-half day week set Saturday afternoons aside for shopping and laundry, but in the evenings and on Sunday there was time for recreation. The Dartmouth guys retrieved some old horseshoes from a dilapidated shed behind the farmhouse and set up pegs in the dirt yard. On the Fourth of July, we borrowed one of the trucks and drove up into the Beartooth Mountains to take in the rodeo at Red Lodge, Montana. On a group picnic one Sunday, we hiked above the snowline and Ned showed off his skill, slaloming down a mushy slope in his hiking boots. This companionship compensated for the strain of having to deal with Jepsen but in the end my Dartmouth buddies got me into the jam that led to my being kicked off the expedition.

The surface of the butte slopes south, then steps down to a smaller section where ants have built two large cone-shaped nests. One day during the lunch break the Dartmouth guys call me over to take a look. They're both carrying shovels.

Ned pushes his blade into one of the nests, removing a small section. We bend over to check out the exposed chambers and pathways which resemble the glassed-in bee colonies some museums have.

Then without warning, Steve rears back and slams his shovel into the nest. "Hey!" I shout. It's like seeing someone get slashed in the face with a razor. I'd assumed that we were going to take the anthill apart in stages so we could scope it out and learn about the structure of the inner maze, but clearly that doesn't interest him.

Steve swings again and sand and ants fly up. The anthill slumps down and hundreds of ants spill from the cracks.

Ned kneels and points to a line of ants hurrying in good order from a hole near the base of the nest. Each insect carries a rice-grain sized pellet in its jaw and, looking closely, we can see inside each pellet the frail shadow of an unborn ant. Sensing a calamity, the nursemaid ants are hoping to salvage the colony's future.

"The idiots don't even know we're here," Ned says.

Steve brings his shovel clanging down on the column, and ants and eggs scatter. Then he smashes the flat of his blade into the base of the nest. Most of the anthill collapses and from the galleries and tunnels in the remaining section thousands of ants come pouring. We all go after the fleeing ants, stomping on them with our boots, and Ned and Steve pound and bang with their shovels, crushing thousands of insects into a kind of paste.

Dust hangs in the air and with the sun beating through it, the top of the butte looks flattened and washed out.

"Think they feel anything?" Steve says as he flicks mangled ants from his blade with a fingernail.

"Nah. They hardly have a nervous system—right, Morgan?" Ned glances over. "Death's just a pinprick to them."

"Well, in that case..." Steve tosses his shovel aside.

The other anthill is still intact and we tear into it, kicking again and again and letting out war-whoops, as a gusty pleasure sweeps through us, a brisk masculine joy. In a matter of seconds, we've just about flattened this one too, and as sand and ants fly up around us, Pete Robinson appears, blinking and gawking, at the far end of the butte.

"What's going on here?" He comes toward us. "Jesus Christ, no!"

Startled, we back away from the ruined anthills.

Pete gapes as if we've suddenly grown tusks and he has no way of communicating with us. He turns and looks back behind him as Jepsen reaches the top of the butte and pauses to catch his breath.

"What the devil...!" Arms pumping, he rushes toward us. He stares at the ruined anthills for a moment, then turns to me.

"Mr. Morgan," he jabs with his finger, "you at least should have known!" But I have no idea what he's talking about.

Using a pair of metal buckets, the professors strain the loose sand through a large-mesh screen, picking off whatever scraps are too big for the mesh, mostly pebbles and twigs. Then with a series of smaller screens, they separate the sand from the tiny bones which the ants have incorporated into their nests. While still in place, the fossils were safe from the weather but now we have to work fast.

The odor of dust and pulverized ants fills my nostrils as I crawl around, looking for tiny bones and teeth and sweeping the sand ahead of me for straining. I feel a strange connection between this tedious job and the earlier work of the ants who've collected these same grains of sand down below and carried them to the top of the butte. I see myself shrunk to the size of an insect, head a black BB, hair-like antennas twitching. At the same time I'm a young man crawling on hands and knees gathering sand, and this peculiar doubleness causes a prickling sensation along my spine as I imagine my panicky relatives fleeing into the badlands to be picked off one by one by birds, lizards and snakes.

Around four o'clock, a thunderhead rolls across the bench and the temperature drops. As a damp breeze swirls up loose sand and dust, we spread tarps over the exposed shale, weighting the corners down with stones, gather our tools and run for the trucks.

We've salvaged a few limbbones, a handful of scattered teeth and one excellent lower jaw an inch and a half long with a couple of molars in place—a dozen fossils in all, about half our usual haul for a week. But of course there's no way of telling how many bones have fallen into crevices, or been crushed or hurled off the side of the butte.

That evening Jepsen informs me that he's called my father and I'm being sent home. When I ask if the Dartmouth guys are going too, he says that they're under the supervision of their own professor and so are not his responsibility. He understands, however, that they've been reprimanded but are being allowed to stay.

On the flight home, I looked over a poem that I'd written during the trip. In slant-rhymed couplets, it seemed like a definite step forward, more skillful than anything I'd done in high school. And I took some relief in the thought that Jepsen was now out of my life. But I felt humiliated as well. It was infuriating that just when he started to come around, I'd screwed up. And I suppose I sensed already that I would have to write about the summer and try to get it all straight in my head. Of course there was no way to foresee what a long-term project that would turn out to be.

In Denver, I switched to a jet and dipped into Dante's *Inferno*. Ciardi's loose terza rima translation was easy to take, but I felt it wasn't quite right for the material. The clever rhymes reminded me of Ogden Nash and an epic descent into Hell ought to have a weightier feel to it. One day, I decided, I would definitely have to tackle the poem in Italian.

POSTCARDS FROM NANCY:
FINDING MY VOICE

As I staggered out of the Quonset hut and stood at a crosswalk near the Old Capital waiting for the light, George Starbuck's brusque question ricocheted around in my head. "Why," he'd just asked at my first conference, holding a batch of my prize-winning undergraduate poems out at arm's length as if they gave off a rancid odor, "are you writing this stuff?"

When the light turned green, I didn't move. Why go on? Somehow I'd deceived myself into thinking I was a poet. Now that was over. The question inflamed my conscience as well, because if my claims as a poet were fraudulent, then hadn't I been leading Nancy on exactly as her parents alleged, luring her into an unsuitable match?

I repeated his words in my mind, shifting the emphasis around to see if I could uncover a glint of hope, and realized that by placing the stress on 'you' ("Why are *you* writing this stuff?"), I could conjure up the suggestion that someone with my strong background and verbal skills could (surely!) do better. But that brief flicker was quickly snuffed, since clearly I would have to start from scratch and discover a whole new way of writing if I wanted to measure up, and in that moment the best part of my life's work, that sheaf of poems he'd just trashed, fluttered around me like brittle leaves and blew off down the street.

Already bald in his mid-thirties, with a shy, sly manner, that brimmed with confidence, Starbuck had dropped out of Cal. Tech. a decade before to devote himself to poetry. A brilliant verbal technician, winner of the Yale Younger Poets Prize, he crafted vivid poems that could embody both farce and tragedy at once. He might, for example, use an acrostic based on a zany pun as the ground for a heartfelt elegy. This sort of game-playing wasn't to everyone's taste, but clearly he was a master of verbal constructions and nobody else around was writing sonnets as hip as his. I tried to tell myself that George just didn't *get* my stuff, but a more sober voice spoke up, asserting that he got it perfectly well but found it completely dismissible.

When the light turned again, I trudged up Washington Street to my Iowa City rooming house. That wide, tree-lined boulevard featured some impressive Victorian homes, at least one of which boasted a fully stocked fall-out shelter in back, but my place was basic. An ancient refrigerator in the second floor hall was the only amenity and when I ate in, I usually warmed up a can of Chef Boyardee ravioli on a one burner hot-plate. Food was far from my mind at the moment, though, as I fell defeated onto my bed.

A couple of acquaintances from my undergraduate writing classes at Harvard had turned up among the host of Workshoppers, and one of them, Bob Grenier, had rented a run-down farmhouse in West Branch, ten miles out of Iowa City, where he and his pregnant wife Emily were living. You had to tromp through a large pig pen to reach their front door, and those Iowa hogs were huge. Bob warned that the sows protecting their piglets could be pretty aggressive, and suggested that I park by the fence on the far side of the pen and he'd come out and escort me across. The pigs snorted and squealed enthusiastically, raising their snouts and hoping for a handout, as Bob, wielding a broom handle, poked and prodded to keep them at a distance while we made our way through the muck.

Behind the house, we strolled through a grove of aging walnut trees, and Bob gathered the fallen nuts in a bag, as we talked about our writing. Trim, athletic, with a blond crew cut, he'd been recruited to Harvard as a basketball player, but the poems of William Carlos Williams, discovered in his freshman year, had set him in a new direction. He'd found his poetic voice early, modeling his work on the Black Mountain poets, Williams' disciples, but he kept in touch with other trends too. When we went inside, he pulled out a well-thumbed copy of *The Tennis-Court Oath*, John Ashbery's most baffling book, full of crazy verbal cut-ups, and introduced me to another, more accessible collection by a little-known Minnesota writer named Bly. Grenier delighted in small epiphanies of language, blinking rapidly and grinning as he pointed to a phrase or an image that struck him as having the true spark. When you hung out with him, you began to take in the world through the eyes of poetry, rather than the other way around, and later in the year, as her pregnancy advanced, Emily would produce an astonishing poem in the combative voice of a mother sow.

ℒ

To brighten my tiny room, I'd pinned the postcards that Nancy sent from Boston to a bulletin board above my desk. She was taking an art history class at Simmons College, and the latest card, from the Gardner Museum, showed a gleaming St. George, confronting a decorative and not very dangerous-looking dragon. Although we planned to marry over Christmas break, everything remained unsettled, with her parents urging us to postpone the wedding at least until June. They argued the delay would give our relationship a more thorough test and allow them time to adjust to the shock of losing Nancy.

June seemed a lifetime away, and now the questions Starbuck raised about my competence as a poet weighed on me as well. How could I draw this person I loved into a dubious marriage when my professional life was menaced with frustration and failure? But steeling myself against these gloomy thoughts, I managed to scribble an encouraging, playful, rather giddy love letter which recast the postcard she'd sent as an allegory of our vexed circumstances. And then, as an afterthought, I copied it over and set it out in lines like a poem, one very different from any I'd written before:

A LETTER IN LATE OCTOBER

My darling, The St. George, whom you gave me in token,
on the wall above my desk weighs with two hands a thin
gold sword, allegorical of December. The dragon of June
has already been probed by the barber pole spear of love,

63

and in the reddish distance under an orange sky, you,
dearest Nancy, kneel beneath the high walls of Simmons
Castle, whence St. George on his blue charger will
carry you to the fertile land of Iowa. The sword is light
in his delicate hands, and his face, as smooth as yours,
is calm, though the shaggy dragon squawks and the horse
rears and turns his head away. I take the postcard down.
The colors are as outlandish as they seemed, and I notice
that Crivelli has perpetrated on both the horse and dragon
rather oversized genitals. That must be part of the story.
A slaty turf and evergreens reinforce the impression
of winter. No more barren or fantastic nights, my wife-to-be.

Hesitantly, not sure it was even a poem, I handed it in to
Starbuck and he inserted it on the class worksheet. With sections
large and impersonal that year, the tone of discussions tended to be
pretty ruthless. We were grad students now and poetry was serious
business. Like dodge-ballers in sixth grade, we finally had the
muscles to raise welts with our well-aimed taunts. Bracing for an
onslaught, I declined to read the poem out loud and asked George
if he'd read it for me. The comments that followed weren't friendly.

"Why is this poetry rather than prose?" one student asked.

"If it's an allegory," someone else piped in, "then who's this
dragon supposed to be? I don't get it."

"I can't see any point to these line-breaks," another student
complained.

Others attacked the personal nature of the writing and
suggested that I ought to check out T.S. Eliot's essay, "Tradition and
the Individual Talent," where the master explains that poetry must
never flaunt the writer's personal emotion.

Starbuck fielded some of the criticisms himself and let others
slide, but I sensed that, in spite of its many flaws, he liked the piece,
so after class, I went up to talk.

"Don't let that guff get to you." He waved a hand toward the
emptying classroom. "Just keep writing like this. You're on the right
track now."

Oddly, this success was almost as worrisome as failure. Having
gained Starbuck's approval once, would I ever be able to do it again?

My doubts accumulated over several weeks until Nancy sent another postcard. This one reproduced a Vermeer interior, and, hoping this time to avoid any questions about whether my response was actually a poem, I composed it in quatrains, tossing in some off-beat line breaks and seeding it with plenty of rhymes.

POSTCARD FROM NANCY

As companion to the Crivelli, a Vermeer
with your sad hand full
of worries on the reverse. This
too from the Gardner:

a young Dutch lady performs at the virginal.
A gallant gentleman, his
back to us, lends one ear
to the music, while

his other attends a blue dressed matron's
account. Inevitably
the checkerboard floor; and
in the left foreground

a bass viol has been laid down next
to a draped desk.
Is he a soldier?
Beside the quill

and parchment, could it be that those
are coins? Why
in such a domestic
scene does Caravaggio's

prostitute laugh on the wall above the music?
This painting filled
with lightly arrested motions
may offer us repose,

in hope that, not in despite of the world,
our music, when I
escort your viola, will hold
us counterpoised.

My diamond for his guilders? No. No brokers, Nancy.
In this age of
war and purchased love
mine's a free answer.

I can't be sure that the workshop approved of this poem any more than the first, but thanks to Starbuck's encouragement, I filtered out some of the guff, and heard a few brighter notes. One of my earlier critics granted that there were commendable formal elements here, although he was puzzled as to exactly what point the long first line in each stanza was trying to make. And in response to the inevitable T.S. Eliot reference, someone pointed out that Robert Lowell and his student Sylvia Plath had used their private experiences and personal emotions in several powerful recent collections. Later in the year, "Postcard from Nancy" would win the university's Academy of American Poets Prize, and after that, a newly married man and prize-winning poet, I could move ahead with confidence.

A Postscript:
By transposing my personal letter into a poem I was able to find my voice, and to this day, when I sense a student is having trouble establishing a voice, I suggest she or he try writing a letter-poem addressed to a lover or a close friend. The intimate tone will give the poem a leg up, and while it doesn't guarantee success it opens fresh possibilities for a personal diction and believable emotional content that can help with whatever the student-poet tries in the future.

THE DOLPHINS OF ATLANTIS

With standing room only in the largest of the Quonset hut classrooms, all the first year graduate students squeezed in and glanced around, aghast at our number—fifty? sixty? How could there be that many promising young poets in an entire nation, much less one remote, corn-fed university town? At the front of the class, George Starbuck, Donald Justice, Marvin Bell and workshop director Paul Engle stared back at us, trying to conceal their dismay. To our instructors, we must have looked like a regiment of the unlikeliest recruits, would-be bards dragooned from urban gin shops, dusty backstreet bookstores, and uncouth cow colleges across the nation and dropped off on their doorstep for basic training in the art. How had this poetic population explosion come about?

That string of Quonset huts on the banks of the Iowa River had served for years as the home of the Writers' Workshop. The corrugated army surplus structures made space on the cheap for a marginal academic enterprise—the graduate creative writing program—which by 1965 had become, even more than football, what the University of Iowa was known for outside of the state.

In mid-September, with the sun beating down on the metal building, the overworked ventilation fan couldn't handle our combined body heat and I hesitate to mention the smell. But our instructors plunged ahead, handing out a sheaf of poems and going over it in gritty detail, trying to show us how to read with a poet's eye, ear, and nose, catching the whiff...I mean the wit...in an unexpected colloquial phrase, marking the formal count of syllables in a line and the way a particular vowel sound could forge a link between stanzas. I remember a couple of poems by Frank O'Hara— one about Lana Turner collapsing, and another asserting that soot is essential to the city's ambiance: "You don't refuse to breathe do you?"

My undergraduate background in close critical reading offered little help with this unconventional fare. It was as if, instead of examining poems with the well-stocked analytical minds of scholars, we now had to make our way with the feelers of insects through a buzzing, twittering meadow of words. Discouraged by the muggy heat, the odor and our unmanageable numbers, our teachers cut the class short and told us that next week we'd be meeting in one of the university's traditional lecture halls, preferably one with air-conditioning.

But why were there so many of us in the first place? This question dangled for months before the answer leaked out.

It seems the previous spring there had been a shake up in the office staff. A secretary had been fired, and in retaliation she'd sent out acceptance letters to every single applicant. The talented, the passable, and the unspeakable, all of us had received the same warm message, praising our writing samples and welcoming us into the program. What's more, with the conflict in Vietnam ratcheting up, a loophole in the draft law offered graduate students, even those in arcane disciplines like creative writing, a military deferment. And so we'd flooded into Iowa City, drawn by an act of secretarial pique and by the escalating war.

When the size of the calamity became apparent, Marvin Bell, a recent Workshop grad with actual military experience, though few publications as yet, was added to the staff and given the job of drill-sergeant. Still in his uniform, he stood modestly to the side at that first class meeting, but later, donning civvies, he took on the program's basic-training course, "Craft of Poetry," and thanks in large part to him this least selective class in Workshop history rounded into shape and produced its share of notable graduates.

Nancy arrived in Iowa City on the coldest night of the year and when I went out to start our aging Peugeot, I was shocked by the frigid air and horrified to find that, at twenty below, the battery was dead. With her plane due in twenty minutes, I phoned the airport and asked if there was a taxi driver who could meet her, a young woman flying in from Boston, and bring her to our apartment.

The woman on the other end called out into the waiting area. A cabby got on the line and I described my wife's trim frame and long brown hair and mentioned that she'd be carrying a musical instrument case.

"What kind of instrument?"

"A viola. It's like a violin but bigger."

He quickly spotted a shivering coed with an abandoned look, stung by the brutal temperature and by my absence, and explained: "Your father's car won't start. He asked me to take you home."

During the weeks of anxious waiting for her arrival, I'd imagined our life together as transformative, mythic, a Wagnerian melding of souls. But marriage trumps romance, and within the first week Nancy pointed out that if she took the trouble to boil peas for dinner, though I'd always hated cooked vegetables, out of consideration for her effort, I should at least try to eat them. And if I wasn't yet capable of doing my share of the cooking, she expected me to pitch in and help with the dishes afterward. She was a full-time student too, but the chores of housekeeping—shopping, laundry, cleaning—fell unequally on her. Up to a point she accepted this extra burden, but when the line was crossed, she let me know and my conscience, as well as my love, rallied to her side. I'd read de Beauvoir's *The Second Sex*, hadn't I?—and was a feminist, at least in theory.

But it's not always possible to foresee the consequences of our theories. Though I'd never done more than heat a can of ravioli before, Nancy showed me how to fry up franks and hamburgers and I began to contribute a couple of meals a week, eventually adding spaghetti to my repertoire and learning to fashion a range of pizzas from the dough she provided. As to blending our lives, there was plenty of that, coordinating our daily class schedules, with concerts, poetry readings and movies thrown in, and plenty of bumping into each other at odd moments for reassuring hugs in our intimate apartment.

But I soon discovered that Nancy had her own ideas about the nature of marriage. At nineteen, she saw a threat in the spiritual merging of identities that I'd looked for. She feared that my more established interests and tastes might overwhelm hers, leaving no room for her to develop as a separate person. In her view, we should be able to spend time apart as happily as together. Why shouldn't she attend a concert of new music while I went to a movie? Or if I wanted to have a few beers with my poet friends, fine—but I should be prepared to drop her off at home first if she had a German test to prepare for or a Chaucer paper to write. Instead of blending into one, she saw us as a linked pair—two people giving each other support but allowing for our separate spheres, like a couple of stars rotating around a common center of gravity, rather than fusing their light into one unstable, massive body of fiery gas.

David Schloss slept late. If I knocked on his door before noon, I might not get an answer or else he'd be in a fog and unable to function. But usually by twelve-thirty or one, he was up—though still in his underwear—when I came by with a draft of my latest poem. Pulling on a pair of black jeans and lacing his boots—the sharp city-kid look he'd brought with him from Brooklyn—he'd pour some cereal in a bowl and, while spooning it in, read over my poem. If it showed any promise, he took out a pencil and framed with thoughtful brackets every superfluous word. Then he read it again and underlined anything that smacked of cliché, lacked clarity, or struck him as "intellectual bullshit" (his critical term of choice).

The early poems of Ezra Pound were Dave's touchstones, and until I could develop the ability to step back and see my own work with sufficient detachment, I relied on his editorial judgment. Dave's editing saved me from embarrassment when my poems came up in workshop, but more important he modeled the craft of revision for me. By watching him work, I was eventually able to internalize his techniques and even now when I look at a student poem or rethink one of my own, I fall back on his critical symbols and categories. As he overhauled a draft, he'd mutter to himself "bullshit…irrelevant…not clear…cliché…nonsense," while on the flip side, his few chary adjectives of praise—"interesting," "moody," or, much more rarely, "cool"—suggested that I was on to something.

In those days, I wrote catch-as-catch-can, but mostly late in the evening, as consciousness loosened its grip and images floated up from the day. But Schloss's creative process was very different. He explained that only by sleeping late could he gain access to deeper layers of thought. He kept a notebook and pencil beside his bed and when he woke from a dream, he'd scribble down whatever images and phrases came into his head. He took dictation from his dream-life, he said, because, when fully awake, his mind tended to operate in critical mode. As a result his poems had a quirky, surreal edge to them, but just what they were about was frequently in question. When they came up in workshop the students and often even the instructor seemed baffled.

One day a poem of his with the seductive title "The Dolphins of Atlantis" appeared on the worksheet, and when the discussion bogged down, feeling a debt of gratitude to my friend and editor, I jumped in and defended it with a careful line-by-line reading. In the rancorous debate that followed, I may have won a few converts, but after the session, David shook his head and told me that my interpretation had nothing to do with what he'd been thinking about when he wrote the thing.

Having been duped by my own ingenuity, I was dumbfounded. But then I had a great idea. Would he mind if I borrowed his title and wrote the poem I'd just described myself? David hesitated, running his fingertips over his temple as he thought. That catchy title was the best thing about his poem, but since I'd just shown my loyalty, if not my critical insight, he shrugged, and said, sure, go ahead.

THE DOLPHINS OF ATLANTIS

As the town walls fell apart
a particle at a time, their arms
contracted, their human contours

sleekened, sinuously, like a shark's.
The face went last, long after
they were swimming in and out of doors.

Their paved streets, water polished,
shine like cast-off necklaces, exciting
fatal plunges from the decks of yachts.

They breathe another logic, simply
understanding that for them, it was easy.
"The final evolution we have become:

loss of feet, of names," a legend
inscribed minutely in the deep
foreheads of those who might remember.

"The Dolphins of Atlantis" turned a corner for my work, stepping away from the clever Ashberyan cut-ups I'd been experimenting with to a more approachable, more lyrical style, and a more inward content. In a way, the dolphins embodied my new aesthetic— alluring, dream-like, a little dangerous—and their mysterious underwater world symbolized the artistic community my friends and I were forming. In that sense, the poem describes our progression from student-poets to the real thing, while transferring our casual coterie from landlocked Iowa City to the mythical ocean deeps.

Jon Anderson and Steve Orlen lived two flights up across the hall from each other, and in our second year in the Workshop their downtown rooming house became our gathering place. Sprawling on ratty chairs and couches, or propped on pillows on the dusty floor, we'd hang out, talking about poetry, movies, sex, what magazines we'd sent our stuff out to and who, among our contemporaries, had made the latest breakthroughs in their writing. This aspect of graduate school, freed from the restraints of classroom discussions, was vital to our development. Though lacking the cafes, museums and great architecture of a major city, as the place where we formed those key friendships and forged our youthful aesthetic, Iowa City was our Paris.

With his wispy blond moustache and brassy Boston accent, Anderson was the magnet. Skinny, funny, original, and an ardent Red Sox fan—his poem, "The Summer Deaths" intones with rue and reverence their starting line-up from his youth—he had a gloomy side too, a moodiness, that gave his personality its edge. Abused as a child, he struggled with depression and had turned to poetry in a passionate quest to uncover—recover—endangered parts of himself. The title of his first collection, *Looking for Jonathan*, alludes to this search. He'd immersed himself in Rilke, scouring the Orpheus sonnets for poetic strategies, and absorbing the *Letters to a Young Poet* as if they'd been written for him. He was generous with advice and clear about his ambition—not for fame which he discounted, but for the next essential poem. If Dave Schoss was our designated critic, Jon was our metaphysician, struggling to crack open the mystery of poetic inspiration and find the alchemy that could make a merely decent poem great.

Insomnia often kept him working through the night, and by morning he'd have run through a dozen drafts and come up with another insight into the poetic process, which he'd pass along at our next gathering. "Love the mysterious," he might argue, lifting his shoulders, spreading his palms in front of him, "don't try to explain it away." And this proposition was likely to spark an extended discussion, as we questioned and elaborated his point. The proof was always in the poems, and we'd pull books of recent poetry from the shelves—Merwin, Bishop, Berryman, Plath—and read out key passages to back up or refute an argument.

Sometimes Anderson would formulate his discoveries as literary axioms ("A quiet steady voice may be the most enduring") or spell them out as practical tips ("Say the hardest thing, but don't stop there—keep the poem going"), and some years later he published a small pamphlet called "Helpful Hints," aimed at beginning poetry students, with fifty-nine of these pointers laid out in numbered order. As Jon saw it, we were engaged in a collective endeavor, and the advances or "breakthroughs" that any one of us made promoted the group effort. And generalizing this view, he contended that poets everywhere, no matter how antisocial or egotistical they might be on the surface, were, at a deeper level, all secretly in cahoots. He acknowledged the competition for recognition and space in the journals but considered those issues secondary. The underlying point, he felt, was that anyone who took the risk of being a poet, who was willing to walk that emotional edge day after day, putting their psyches on the line, was engaged in the visionary project of advancing our mutual aesthetic and spiritual understanding. This generous insight took some of the sting out of the brutal critiques we often faced in Workshop and we all bought in to it, although later on, out in the literary world, it disconcerted me to see how fragmented and contentious the poetic landscape had become and how many contemporaries hadn't begun to grasp Jon's point.

Not that we always adhered to it ourselves. Since we saw our calling as central to the advancement of the human spirit, any poet who failed to live up to the highest standards, or who'd backed off in a recent collection from earlier achievements was seen as copping out. Even a very good poem that merely repeated an earlier triumph risked falling into the trap of formula and, though we admired verbal skills and formal virtuosity wherever we found them, without the right vision and sensibility, technique was never enough. Clever poets who hoped to pun or sass their way to Parnassus were scorned as ducking the essential task.

Though this spiritual quest may sound intimidating, Jon believed that playfulness was an important part of the job. Like a kid choosing his ideal lefty line-up, he enjoyed comparing lists of favorite formal or free verse poems, favorite collections, favorite movies, favorite directors, and, in another vein, he and a friend once spent a couple of weeks developing "The Game of Iowa City," a cross between Monopoly and Shoots and Ladders. Players threw dice and landed on squares with instructions like, "*The New Yorker* rejects your best poem—go back 3 spaces," or "A 'famous writer' pukes on your couch—advance 2." It had, I seem to recall, a set of "Get Out of Town" cards, with messages like, "Your car breaks down in Davenport, go back 4 spaces" and "Your plane circles O'Hare for 3 hours, go back 1." The object of the game was to reach the final square and "Get out of Iowa City," but the board was arranged so that this outcome was not just difficult to achieve but virtually impossible. Mirroring a poet's life of endless existential struggle, the game was a triumph in its conception but a serious downer in practice, and those who actually played it found that it soon brought on a state of hair-pulling frustration verging on despair.

Anderson was always trying to extend his range. He relished stories of oddball behavior—like one about a prisoner who was obsessed with eating glass—and often these tabloid squibs would be turned into metaphor and slotted into his work. When stuck for inspiration, he'd scan the dictionary, noting down words that carried a cargo of poetic implications. Soon you'd find them

74

cropping up in his work: *odalisque, contemplative, medallion, solicitude, retrospect*. And when completely blocked, he had another recourse, one however that didn't make it into "Helpful Hints." I once visited an introductory writing class he was teaching and heard him advise the group, which included a couple of nuns, that when he needed fresh ideas he found it useful to masturbate.

Although majoring in English, Nancy kept up her music, taking viola lessons and playing in several groups. In addition to frequent concerts, we saw scores of movies, bowled occasionally, and attended lots of poetry readings. Now and then, the readings were accompanied by a pig roast. To be fully cooked, the sacrificial hog was supposed to be buried in a pit of hot coals overnight, but for Allen Ginsberg's visit there was a mix-up, and, after chanting a couple of sutras, reading one long incomprehensible poem, and OM-ing at us for half an hour, the poet invoked his kosher upbringing and took a pass on a slice of bloody pork.

On another occasion we were invited to a more formal dinner for John Berryman, where, Nancy noted with concern that his wife's primary task was to ply him with cups of coffee in hopes of sobering him up in time for the reading. Her every other sentence throughout the meal was, "Drink your coffee, John." He wasn't the only soused poet to come through town (and in his case the tipsiness suited his idiosyncratic style), but the strangest performance we saw was given by Lawrence Ferlinghetti who flew in from the Coast on acid and spent most of his reading trying to describe the amazing cloud formations he'd encountered on the flight and insisting that if we could only experience what he had, our lives would be altered and our earth-bound souls redeemed.

We were avid movie buffs and a buddy of Dave Schloss's, a grad student in film, had access to all the flicks that came into Iowa City for their various classes. On weekends we'd often spend from eight in the evening to two or three a.m. screening these movies in our own private film festival, and I must have seen more movies in those few years than in all of my life up to that point. *Jules and Jim, Breathless, Last Year at Marienbad*, and *Children of Paradise* became our benchmarks for serious art, but we didn't scorn Hollywood thrillers, musical comedies or campy horror flicks either.

This crash program in cinema led a couple of us to sign up for a beginning film-making course which culminated with each student producing a five minute short. My take on a boozy loner living among rats in the attic of an abandoned Iowa City railroad station starred Jon Anderson, and Nancy and I had parts in his short about a ghostly love triangle spiced with hints of murder and incest. Working hard in the editing room, I pasted scraps of black and white 16 mm. film into some semblance of a story, but my best efforts turned out to be more like a parody of a student film than the gripping psychological study I'd intended.

Still, the physical nature of snipping and gluing film and the startling juxtapositions that can be achieved as shots and scenes are moved around, taught me something about the creative process. In the editing room, a film can be stopped and examined one frame at a time, or speeded up so that minutes flash by in seconds. A freeze frame holds a single image up for contemplation while jump-cuts push the story ahead with a nervous urgency. The poet Muriel Rukeyser, who worked professionally as a film editor, compares that work to the poet's in her book-length meditation, *The Life of Poetry*: "The editor in the cutting room is dealing in time, in rhythms of length and relationship. The selection and ordering are a work of preparation and equilibrium, of the breaking of the balance and the further growth. The single image, which arrives with its own speed, takes its place in a sequence which reinforces that image."

The only Chinese restaurant in town served chop suey out of cans and most of the better places were beyond our means, so we often found ourselves eating in the student cafeteria. One day, Dave Schloss pointed to a striking young woman and remarked that he'd noticed her several times before. Tall and thin, with high cheekbones, and long chestnut hair flowing down her back, she had a sophisticated look that set her apart from most of the coeds on campus. Dave speculated about her major, which turned out to be art, and commented that she always seemed to be by herself or with a group of friends, rather than hanging out with any particular guy. But of course this might just mean that she had a boyfriend back home, wherever that was.

"Why don't you introduce yourself?" we said.

He hesitated, but eventually gave in and after they started going together, we learned that Penelope was well aware of her beauty, but saw it as no great asset. Before taking up art, she'd been a serious piano student, and had come in second in a concerto competition at the Aspen Music Festival. Afterwards one of the judges told her that she actually played better than the guy who'd won, but the committee had voted to give him first prize because it might nail down a recording contract for him and, in any case, was sure to advance his career; whereas they figured that a beautiful young woman like Penelope was destined to get married, have kids and give up performing. This explanation, meant to console her, made her furious. She brooded over it for months and, when she regained her equilibrium, abandoned the piano and took up art.

When she spoke to you, Penelope stared aggressively into your eyes, not letting you look away. Everything she said was emphatic. If it wasn't important why would she bother to say it? Her painting technique, on the other hand, was unhurried and methodical, as she painstakingly selected her colors and built up layers of pigment to mask the thousands of brushstrokes and produce a polished, idealized surface.

In my third year at Iowa, I'd been assigned to teach an introductory poetry writing course and one day a young man from the class came by the small office I shared with another teaching assistant. A new four story brick structure had replaced the legendary Quonset huts as home for the Writers Workshop, and the furniture, all bright and shiny, seemed more appropriate to junior executives at IBM, we thought, than to hot young writing prospects like ourselves.

After going over my student's poems one by one, I told the him that I thought his work was impressive, especially for a freshman, a bit heavy on the adjectives perhaps, but well beyond what the other students in the class were doing.

"I know that," he said, "but what I need you to tell me is—do I really have it? Can I make it as a writer?"

Although I'd had a few decent publications and the encouragement of my teachers, that same question hung in the air for me. I told him what I still believe, that becoming a writer hinges on making discoveries for yourself about language and also about yourself, *breakthroughs* call them, and nobody can tell you in advance when they will happen. Teachers can only try to assist the process.

But he restated his question. He mentioned that he was a military kid who'd grown up in Germany, Japan and Washington, D.C., and had only a slight connection to Iowa—an uncle on a farm somewhere. But he'd heard from this uncle that the university had a creative writing program and that's why he'd come here: "I had to find out if I could make it as a writer."

He ran a hand back through his hair and then sat still, tilted slightly forward, holding his breath and waiting for me to offer up a judgment. It seemed as though at that moment the wrong word might stop him cold and the right one launch him like an arrow arching over the cornfields into the bull's eye of a Pulitzer Prize.

So I looked his poems over again. It would involve hard work, I told him, but I saw no reason to discourage him. "If you really want to write, you should keep at it, since it's clear that you have some talent." And with that key word, *talent*, I sensed his taut body relaxing, filling with massive relief. So I pushed the point a bit further: "If you have the ambition and stuck to it," I told him, "I don't see why you can't make it as a writer."

His face flushed. "That's really great to hear!" And grinning earnestly, Denis Johnson reached over to shake my hand, partly from gratitude, it seemed, but also to clinch the deal.

LABORS LOST AND FOUND

In the fall of 1972, as articles detailing the break-in at the Watergate and other impeachable offenses appeared in the Long Island paper *Newsday*, Nancy and I signed up to work for the Democratic presidential campaign. Volunteering at McGovern's storefront headquarters in Southold, we joined a motley group of anti-war liberals and old-line union folk sitting at rickety picnic tables and making phone calls aimed at winning over independent voters and keeping up the spirits of the few registered Democrats in our disproportionately Republican county. Occasionally, challenged by backers of the president, I found myself making impassioned speeches about our misguided propping up of a brutal and incompetent regime in Saigon. To no effect, of course. It was disillusioning to see how little impact Nixon's crimes and the continuing war had on that election. But by the next summer, the public had caught on and the Senate Watergate hearings riveted everyone's attention.

That summer we were on the move. Nancy had been hired to direct a preschool in Yorktown Heights, and since housing in Westchester County was beyond our means, we scouted further north, out of commuting range of New York, and settled on a scruffy farmhouse with lots of character in the village of Kent Cliffs. Downtown Kent Cliffs consisted of a tiny general store next to a combination antique shop and real estate office. That was it. But we furnished our house with cut-rate "antiques," and a pleasant twenty minute drive around a pair of reservoirs brought us to Carmel, which had a shopping center and Morettini's, a variety store with stairs leading up, down and around to additional niches filled with more and more offbeat and occasionally handy stuff.

Our house had its own oddities. When it rained, water gushed through the crude stone walls into the basement, where it was gathered into channels, directed to a cistern and removed by a sump pump. Our property backed on a pond which emptied into one of the reservoirs and we joked that New York City's celebrated drinking water took its distinctive bouquet from having passed through our cellar.

The previous owner, the town's volunteer fire chief, had parked his engine in the front yard. He'd also set up a one lane bowling alley in the basement, to which cold beer was delivered through a plastic tube rigged from a keg in the kitchen fridge. The bowling alley and fire engine were gone but a sun porch that he'd converted into a paneled office remained, and that's where I set up shop. I wrote mornings and after lunch painted the outside trim and dealt with the rocks and rabbits that plagued our vegetable garden. Meanwhile, Nancy stripped off four or five layers of faded wallpaper in the upstairs bedrooms and painted the walls.

We were now feeling settled enough to start thinking about expanding our family and that meant it was my turn to apply for a teaching job. There were only a handful of colleges within driving distance, however, and none of them seemed to be looking for a creative writer.

At the beginning of her second trimester, Nancy suffered a miscarriage. Her obstetrician downplayed its significance, suggesting that the lost embryo might have been deformed, in which case it was better that the pregnancy went no further. He encouraged us to try again. But for Nancy the developing child was not just a jumble of cells. At night, she lay awake grieving over its death and even now, over forty years later, she sometimes finds herself distracted by thoughts about the person it might have grown up to be. My response at the time was to turn my grief into a poem.

SONNET OF THE LOST LABOR

Comes a day at high spring when everything gluts.
The globules of fat within each cell burst
open and the ecstatic heat, seeding the air
with the damp odor of birth, oozes among the grass.

Came a voice like yours, calling me up the stairs
to where you sat in the bathroom, shaken,
leaking the blood our child had nested in.
I hug you again and feel your pain, lost labor:

the ache of birth six months too soon;
but as I approach that moment's stain, my eyes
haze over, my head begins to float.
At the sight of its blood, death red, sight
fails. You catch the little monster in a cup, save
it for the lab. Christ, Nancy, I am not so brave.

In other ways, too, our plans weren't working out. Although
several schools brought me to campus for interviews, I hadn't
landed a job. We still wanted a child though, and Nancy took a
leave of absence from school to help her sustain her next
pregnancy. But with no money coming in, we were soon living
day to day.

At a low point, I visited the unemployment office in Peekskill
to find out if I was eligible for assistance. But since I hadn't earned
a salary in years, I learned that I was not, as far as the government
was concerned, legitimately unemployed. This led me to wonder
what role, if any, poets have in the larger economy, the network of
associations that turns work into products, products into money
and money into food and housing. In that chain, our poorly
requited output pointed away from salaried labor, filling the gap
with something less material which has no standing in the world
of finance and business.

Only a handful of poets make their living from sales or by
giving public readings. More commonly we have to find day-jobs.
In an earlier generation T. S. Eliot worked in a bank, hating every
minute of it, while Wallace Stevens was a successful insurance
executive and William Carlos Williams earned his living as a
doctor. Teaching was another solution but with such jobs now
scarce, I'd recently heard of some poets who'd taken up a less
savory enterprise. To pay the rent they signed on to write straight

or gay or S & M "stroke-books." Working in tiny cubicles, they churned out a novel a week, each written to a predetermined outline, with the specified sex acts coming at set intervals—one every five or six pages. What's more, if their product was any good, they could expect to gather a following and receive the kind of encouraging fan-mail (addressed to their punning pen-names) that most poets only dream about.

Apparently, the society I lived in valued pornography over poems—a discouraging thought—, but I wondered if that was the whole story. I recalled the bulky anthology of English and American poetry that I'd pored over during adolescence as I tried to find my bearings, hoping that my own writing might someday serve others in the same way. Back then I'd assumed that wealth and fame would follow. But in fact poems aren't merchandise. Instead, as Lewis Hyde proposes in his book *The Gift*, they're a speculative offering to the future, and unlike the chain that leads from product to cash, poets link into a more spiritual chain looking back to the writers of the past whom we value and learn from and ahead to our own future readers. Poems are like messages in bottles hurled into the sea from a cliff and we may never know when one reaches some distant shore and is taken into a reader's heart.

Not having landed a job in my first go-round, for a second year I sent out applications. My new poems were starting to attract interest from magazines, including *The New Yorker*, which eventually published two of them, and I took encouragement when Vassar College invited me to campus for a lunchtime interview. They weren't looking for a creative writer, however, just checking me out as someone who lived in the area and might help with a lower-level writing section if the need arose.

Then in mid-January a junior faculty member resigned unexpectedly, and they called. Would I be willing to take on his two sections? Classes started the next week. I said that would be no problem.

Elated at being employed at last, I enjoyed everything about the job—students, colleagues, even the forty minute commute through rural Putnam and Duchess counties. In mid-semester I joined several faculty poets, including Nancy Willard and Eamon Grennen, in a campus reading and afterwards I was taken aback when someone from the audience came up and asked: "Are you *the* John Morgan?" At first I was tempted to deny it, but he explained that he'd seen my work in magazines and in the Paul Carroll anthology, *The Young American Poets*. So apparently the cloak of invisibility surrounding me wasn't as impenetrable as I'd thought.

On one of our early visits to Morettini's, I'd purchased a journal, a tall book with a blue cover and "Record" embossed in gold on the spine. In it I wrote down what I'd been doing and thinking in an unorganized, unpolished way, and when I'd filled that book up, I bought its matching twin, in red. Here is the entry for April 26, 1976:

Woke up around 7:15 yesterday morning. N. moving around, opening dresser drawers, in and out of the room. Packing for the hospital. Her contractions had begun at 6. Neither of us quite believed it. False labor, we thought. But went ahead timing, breathing. Called Dr. Robertson around 8. He a bit skeptical, but said to call again if the contractions intensified and gradually they did. Called Linda Klocker, our Lamaze instructor. On learning the contractions had lengthened past 60 seconds in some cases, she urged us to call Robertson again and he said to come on down.

We left home at about 1:10 with a Lamaze bag containing two tennis balls, wash cloth, lollypop, a pillow and a peanut butter sandwich. I drove cautiously and N. continued her breathing. By now the pain was quite intense and she had rectal pressure and occasionally an urge to push. But since the intervals between contractions remained approximately 5 minutes, I persisted in the belief that she was just moving from early to active phase.

At the hospital she requested a wheel chair, feeling unable to walk and while she was taken upstairs and prepped, I parked the car and showed our insurance forms to the woman in 'Admitting.' When I reached the labor room, N. was writhing through frequent intense contractions. The nurse who prepped her discovered her in advanced active phase, entering transition. She was 8 centimeters dilated. Dr. Robertson who'd just completed an earlier delivery was called from lunch and arrived to find N. ready to give birth. She'd spend no more than 20 minutes in the labor room, and the four of us, nurse, doctor, patient, and husband moved quickly to the delivery room.

I capped and masked with the doctor while the nurse worked with N. Soon she was pushing. In the mirror reflecting her I saw blood oozing and as she pushed her face turned scarlet and she cried out at the pain. It was about now I began to feel faint. Doctor and nurse noticed my condition and said I should leave the room if I was in trouble, but I sat down and stayed.

The long needle of novocain for her episiotomy did not ease my condition, but now birth was near and I could see Nancy's bottom swelling out with the baby's head. In my excitement my head cleared and I could stand up again. A quarter-sized chunk of the baby's scalp was showing. I tried to comfort and encourage Nancy with this news, as did the doctor and nurse, but her pain was extreme and she was probably beyond our reach.

Like a small coconut it came, bit by bit, and then the head was out, blue and dazed. Now the worst was over for N. The baby twisted slightly and the shoulders came and then he was out. Other nurses had arrived with a heated tray for the newborn. The doctor used a suction device to clear the mucous from his mouth and nasal passages. We had decided on Jeffrey for a boy, so Jeffrey it was, breathing now and color beginning to come, turning blue to orange, as he let out his first screams.

Dr. Robertson placed him on Nancy's chest and he quieted and struggled to open his eyes. Nancy, dazed herself, stared at the stranger. Then he was moved to the heated bed and Dr. Robertson began to sew Nancy up.

The entry for June 1, 1976 is much shorter. It reads: *"This evening I accepted a one year appointment in the English Dept. of the University of Alaska. This should be interesting."*

III.

FEELINGS INTO FORMS

A FORMAL FEELING

Emily Dickinson: #341

After great pain, a formal feeling comes—
The Nerves sit ceremonious, like Tombs—
The stiff Heart questions was it He, that bore,
And Yesterday, or Centuries before?

The Feet, mechanical, go round—
Of Ground, or Air, or Ought—
A Wooden way
Regardless grown,
A Quartz contentment, like a stone—

This is the Hour of Lead—
Remembered, if outlived,
As Freezing persons, recollect the Snow—
First—Chill—then Stupor—then the letting go—

A formal feeling. You've survived, but in the mind it's not over. This is a poem about romantic devastation. Interestingly, it's also about poetry. "The Feet, mechanical, go round," seems to describe its own plodding pace. And "A Quartz contentment," seems for a moment to overcome the tragic mood—it's a glimmer of what a poem might be, a crystallization of that mood. The poem even has a moment of sly humor in it—"was it He, that bore—" Humor is another way to master a romantic devastation.

Of course in lyric poetry the emotion doesn't have to be tragic. Wordsworth works it out for happier feelings, in his daffodils poem, remember: "I wandered lonely as a cloud…?" He ends that poem:

For oft when on my couch I lie
in quiet or in pensive mood
they flash upon the inward eye
which is the bliss of solitude
and then my heart with pleasure fills
and dances with the daffodils.

Wordsworth's poem may at first seem to be an outburst of spontaneous joy, but there's more to it. We know for instance that the opening line of the poem, "I wandered lonely as a cloud," is simply not true. We know this because we have the journal written by his sister Dorothy which describes the same incident. She was there too, and so Wordsworth's isolation is an invention. Of course he could have said, "We wandered lonely as two clouds," but poetic license took over, thank goodness, from the literal truth.

And it's worth recalling how Wordsworth defined the lyric poem: "emotion recollected in tranquility." When the feelings are actually happening, they're too strong in us and we live them, but can't write them down. It's only later, lying on your couch in a pensive mood, that a poem may get started.

Sometimes we can force a poem by giving ourselves an assignment or writing down whatever pops into our head. But for now I want to get at a certain psychological truth about poetry. In the first chapter, I mentioned that Robert Frost called lyric poetry: "a momentary stay against confusion," and quoted from an article in *The American Poetry Review*, where Gregory Orr spelled this out in more detail. Here's the full quote:

"Our day-to-day consciousness can be characterized as an endlessly-shifting, back-and-forth awareness of the power and presence of disorder in our lives and our desire or need for a sense of order. Most of us live most of our lives more or less comfortably with the daily interplay of these two awarenesses, but in certain existential crises, disorder threatens to overwhelm us entirely and in those cases, the very integrity of the self is threatened, and its desire or ability to persist is challenged. Among the most obvious and dramatic of these upheavals we could include intense romantic passion or the sudden death of someone near and dear to us. And yet our instability is present to us almost daily in our unpredictable moods and the way memories haunt us and fantasies play themselves out at will on our inner mental screens. We are creatures whose volatile inner lives are both mysterious to us and beyond our control. How to respond to the strangeness and unpredictability of our own emotional being? One important answer to this question is the personal lyric, the 'I' poem dramatizing inner and outer experience."

Orr gives as an example a traumatic event from his own childhood, when he killed his brother in a hunting accident. It took him years to begin to come to grips with the guilt he felt, but poetry, when he discovered it in high school, was an important part of the healing process.

Let me give an example from my own experience. In November 1993, without warning, our son Ben went into a coma. He had to be medevacked to Seattle, and for five days we didn't know if he would ever come out of it and if he did what shape he would be in. During that time I made myself write. I did it partly to get some kind or control over my feelings, and also to keep in touch with the writerly part of myself that I felt in danger of losing.

I wrote sonnets, because the tight fourteen line form gave me a greater sense of control. I don't normally write in form, I write in free verse. But during this time the formal challenge helped me get things out and onto the page. I should also say that I knew at the time that those poems were not any good. I was writing them purely for myself, as therapy, to keep myself steady and objectify the chaos of my inner feelings. But a couple of years later, after Ben had recovered from his initial illness and was dealing with its long-term effects, I was ready to go back and write about our experiences thinking I might write them up as a memoir.

But looking over the poems I'd written at the time, I found that some of them were salvageable, and others reminded me of details that I could use to make new poems about that experience. Out of this came the sequence *Spells and Auguries*. These are not tight sonnets. The rhyming is only occasional and I loosened the form by introducing dropped lines—that is, breaking some lines in each poem in half, so the poems don't have that square, boxy sonnet look. But they were all originally fourteen lines long and the best of them have a true sonnet feel of powerful emotions being controlled by form.

There are twenty-four poems in all, covering about five years. Here are three that deal with the first few days of Ben's illness.

SIRENS AND FLASHING LIGHTS

November 8, 1993, 7 A.M.

Your cry, half howl, half moan, rocks us awake.
We rush in, find you
                                lurching out of control,
eyes fixed and fingers crimped—our son, eleven,
healthy yesterday. Your body twitches, sways.
Nancy's about to faint, so I say, "Sit ,"
and press her head between
                                        her knees, then phone
for help. She throws things in a bag, sensing
already that our lives have changed.

I call again and scream at the dispatcher.
"They're on their way," she says, concerned. Our common
thought: your brain in pieces like a shattered
glass, you may
                                never find yourself again.
Sirens and flashing lights intensify
our sense of helplessness as help arrives.

SLEEPLESS TO SEATTLE: NANCY

November 10

I wore my parka with two blankets over
like a mummy and they kept asking how
I was and I'd say,
                                'How is he?' and they'd say,
'Doing great!' but the oxygen wasn't flowing
on the plane so they had to pump this bellows

90

thing by hand to keep
                    him breathing and
I hadn't slept for two days and couldn't stop
my shivers. I must've been in shock.

Then at the hospital, all hell broke loose.
They crushed in all at once—the specialists—
to hook him up
                    and get their systems going
and one of them came over to me yelling,
'Christ—why didn't you bring him sooner?'
as though Fairbanks was right around the corner.

INTENSIVE CARE

November 13

The delicate hiss of the pump pulling
phlegm from your chest, green
                    scribbles on the screen
snaking up and down, and a nurse on
permanent duty who says just ignore
those stats and look at the calm sleeping face
of the boy with the tube up his nose, the drip
in his arm and
                    the probe screwed into his skull
gauging pressure on the brain—just watch

his steady breathing. Something is there
inside that was almost taken away,
something coiled and firm waits for another
day, to stick out his tongue on command
and open his
                    bleary eyes and when asked,
"Who is that?" to say, "Why that's my dad."

A hundred years ago, reacting against the artificiality of Romantic Period practices, Ezra Pound said a number of very smart things about writing poetry and "making it new." Poems, he argued, should be composed using only natural words in their natural order, avoiding awkward inversions like "the sky blue." They should include no words that don't contribute to the presentation, i.e. nothing merely decorative. He stressed the importance of the image as a basic unit in poetry (as opposed to rhyme and meter) and he famously intoned: "Go in fear of abstraction."

There's one other Poundian pronouncement that I call to mind when I'm writing a lyric poem: "Only emotions endure." Pound was a conscientious craftsman and he didn't mean that you could pour raw emotions onto the page and expect them to last. The craft has to be there too. But in the long run a well-made poem that lacks an emotional punch is not likely to be remembered.

In a sense, then, the raw material of poetry—in addition to words, of course, is emotion. Sometimes the emotion can be stated directly, but often it needs to find an image to carry it. The image is what transfers it into the reader's mind. Dickenson knew this well, and so she ends her poem of romantic devastation with an image, the hypothermic "chill—then Stupor—then the letting go—"

THE WALK POEM

Walking is good exercise. And for the poet, it can provide the occasion for a meditation that will bring new insights, and a fuller sense of the self in its relationship to the world. Wordsworth sometimes took walks of many days, composing as he went. In a comment on his famous "Lines Composed a few Miles above Tintern Abbey," he said, "I began it upon leaving Tintern, after crossing the Why, and concluded it just as I was entering Bristol in the evening."

The rhythm of walking provides a physical equivalent to meter, though "walk poems" can be written in free verse as well. Either way, the repetitive step after step motion can stimulate the mind to greater awareness, greater intensity. There is the story of Wallace Stevens, deep in thought, composing poems as he walked to the insurance company in Hartford, Connecticut where he worked. An observer noticed him taking a step to one side, as if avoiding a puddle. But there was no puddle—no obstruction at all—except perhaps in Stevens' mind as he deleted an unnecessary adjective and walked on.

Whether poetry is the way you make order out of experience or simply a way to reflect the chaos, this exercise provides a frame. What goes inside it is your own walk. Here are the steps to writing a walk poem:

STEP ONE: Take a walk. The location for the walk can be urban or rural, familiar or new. The important thing is to cultivate a mental alertness to what is around you and to what you're thinking. What comes in fresh through the poet's senses can be passed on as a gift to the reader. If something catches your eye—a car on blocks, a tree with a double trunk—give it sustained attention. Let phrases come to you describing it and what it makes you think.

STEP TWO: This is an exercise in noticing and thinking and also in noticing what you are thinking. So what are you thinking? I mean really—are you thinking that "nature is beautiful," or are you recalling some aggravating incident on the job? Is there a sick friend that you're worrying about or some international crisis? The mind is not limited to the perceptions of the present moment. And if you're simply thinking "nature is beautiful"—face it, you're probably not going to get a poem out of this particular walk.

STEP THREE: Compose a poem based on your walk. Not just what you saw, but the whole experience of it, thoughts and all. As you write feel free to develop those thoughts. Now it's the poem that counts and you'll have to use all your skills to shape it so that the reader can participate fully. Everything that happened on the walk is raw material, but just because it happened doesn't mean that you have to include it if it doesn't seem to advance your poem. Similarly, as you write, feel free to elaborate (read: invent), because now it's the poem and its larger implications that count, not the history of one particular walk.

The kind of poem that results depends on your poetic sensibility and formal concerns. Perhaps it will be a pure lyric like Wordsworth's "I Wandered Lonely as a Cloud," or a playful and fantastic narrative like Elizabeth Bishop's "The End of March." It may be as loose-limbed and zany as what Frank O'Hara called "my I-do-this I-do-that poems" or as tightly crafted as Robert Frost's sonnet "Design," which focuses, you may remember, on a sardonic little tableau involving a spider, a flower, and a moth. I'm assuming the incident recounted in "Design" happened on a walk, since the poet is out in the woods, but no other details of the walk are included. Paradoxically, Frost's "The Road Not Taken" seems to be more of an invented situation than a true walk poem, because here the occasion and presentation are largely symbolic.

The walk poem is open to a number of variations. If instead of walking you prefer to jog or bike or cross-country ski, there may be a poem for you in these activities. Driving a car doesn't work as well since your attention needs to be focused on the road. But any activity involving a gradual movement through the landscape, as long as it gives you scope for fresh observation and thought, can be the source for poems.

Here's a poem of mine which fits the basic pattern. I'm not alone on the walk, but that's ok: neither was Wordsworth when he stumbled on those daffodils.

AN EASY DAYHIKE, MT. RAINIER

for Nancy, Jeff and Ben

Bright mushroom clouds of yellow lilies flame
at Eunice Lake where under jutting peaks,
we snack and muse on Jeff, our older son,

who studies poetry, the climbing art that twines
the word with time, then note fresh deer tracks in
the mud as switchbacks steepen into blueberries.

The lookout tower's locked but we can see
through glass, a gas stove, bunks, a log book
(1986-93),

as drizzle comes. We linger, hoping
that the mountains will de-cloud and talk about
Ben's seizures, never tamed—a recent one

that spun him down the hall, whirled him into
a concrete wall. The school nurse found him
on the floor, knocked cold. I got the call and

in her office—blood dribbled from his nose,
beside his eye a crimson bruise, one tooth
a vicious fang, one broken straight across,

he sat and hardly moved. The razor ridge
to Tolmie Peak, we skip, and so descend
through old-growth deliquescing under rain.

At Eunice Lake again, the deer himself
stares back across his shoulder at our stares.
Later, Ben's dentist sealed the pulp, squeezed

plastic from a tube to patch the cracked
stalactites in his mouth. Headache gone,
he took it patiently, while black light

hardened plastic into tooth, or almost tooth.
As we approach the trailhead, sun breaks through.
A rainbow lies on Mowich Lake. It floats

beneath our feet—a sign perhaps, though who
believes in signs? The world is flux, each day
a setting forth. Our trip's a cache of weathers

like the sky. Six hours into this 'easy
hike,' wasted and refreshed, we reach the rented
Sunray, drink our Diet Cokes and split a peach.

"TRAVELING THROUGH THE DARK": A DIRECTED READING

Faced with a roomful of students interested in making poems, as preparation for the writing I like to toss them into the pool and get them wet. We start by looking at a well-crafted poem, for instance William Stafford's "Traveling Through the Dark," and try to think it through. What choices did the poet have and given those options, how did he decide? Reading inevitably precedes writing, and unless you can find suitable models and begin to read like a writer, your work is likely to be lacking in craft.

After the students look the poem over themselves, I read it out loud, and then start asking questions. I avoid the general all-purpose question, because if I ask, "What's going on here?", I'm likely to get a bunch of puzzled looks. Then one of the brighter students in the class may offer a tentative "reading" of the poem. But that's not what I'm after. I want the students to dig inside the poem, to start thinking locally, and figuring out what the poet herself/himself might have been thinking about in writing it. Of course every word in a poem can be questioned, but not all words are equal. Not all line-breaks are equal, either.

Here's the poem:

TRAVELING THROUGH THE DARK

Traveling through the dark I found a deer
dead on the edge of the Wilson River road.
It is usually best to roll them into the canyon:
that road is narrow; to swerve might make more dead.

By glow of the tail-light I stumbled back of the car
and stood by the heap, a doe, a recent killing;
she had stiffened already, almost cold.
I dragged her off; she was large in the belly.

My fingers touching her side brought me the reason—
her side was warm; her fawn lay there waiting,
alive, still, never to be born.
Beside that mountain road I hesitated.

The car aimed ahead its lowered parking lights;
under the hood purred the steady engine.
I stood in the glare of the warm exhaust turning red;
around our group I could hear the wilderness listen.

I thought hard for us all—my only swerving—,
then pushed her over the edge into the river.

Ok, so you've read the poem to yourself. Now read it again out loud.

Are you ready? In this exercise, I'm going to give my questions first in the form of a list. Then I'll go back and suggest some answers. My questions and answers are only partial, of course. You may be able to think of better ones yourself. But hopefully mine will suggest a writerly approach that will help you worm your way under the poem's skin.

1. Stafford might have started the poem: "Traveling through the dark I found a dead/deer…" What is the effect of holding back the word "dead" till the start of the second line?
2. Why does Stafford specify the Wilson River Road? Do we really care about the name of the road?
3. What does the third line ("It is usually best to roll them into the canyon") tell us about the narrator of the poem? Can you describe the tone of voice here?
4. At the start of the second stanza he "<u>stumbles</u> back of the car." What does the word "stumble" suggest?
5. In the next line he calls the deer a "heap" and then "a doe." How do these words affect your response to the situation?

6. What does the phrase "large in the belly" indicate? Why do you think Stafford puts it that way?

7. The commas around the word "still" in line 11 give it special emphasis, as each comma creates a brief pause. Why do you suppose it's set off like that?

8. In line 12, why does the speaker hesitate?

9. The fourth stanza is largely devoted to a description of the scene. What senses are evoked? What details of the description are particularly striking? What is the speaker doing during this stanza?

10. The last line of the stanza introduces a larger element into the scene. Could you ever actually "hear the wilderness listen"? How does this line influence your response to the poem?

11. The speaker refers in this line to "our group" and in the next he says he "thought hard for us all." Who is the group and who does "us all" refer to? Are they the same thing?

12. Why does the last line of the poem seem anticlimactic? What alternative ending were you looking for?

I hope you've looked over the poem and tried to answer the questions. It's not so much a matter of right and wrong answers but of digging more deeply into the work. Now I'll offer some possible answers. See how they match up with yours.

1. In the first line, as far as we know, that deer is alive. The word "dead" coming as the first word in the second line gets extra emphasis. (Technically, it gets a strong accent as it starts off the line and is followed by two lightly accented words.) The effect is to shock us in the way that finding the dead deer might have shocked the speaker.

2. *The Wilson River Road* is the sort of detail which suggests that the incident actually happened in a particular place at a particular time. Once, when I mentioned that Stafford lived in Oregon, a student in my class said with surprise, "Oh, I know that road!" But this doesn't necessarily mean that the poem is entirely factual, just that Stafford wants us to believe that it is.

3. In the third line, the speaker seems pretty confident that he knows how to handle the situation. He knows the protocol. The tone of the line is casual, colloquial—like some ordinary guy talking—rather than lyrical or conventionally poetic.

4. Stafford could have written "I made my way back of the car." The fact that the speaker "stumbles" is an indication that things

99

may not be going as planned. If we were looking for someone completely on top of the situation, a conventional hero of some sort, maybe he isn't it.

5. In line 6, there's a big tonal shift from "heap" to "doe." The deer is suddenly personalized as we see her close up.

6. "Large in the belly" takes this even further. We are there with the speaker. We know what he knows and suspect what he suspects. When he touches the doe's side and feels its warmth the sense of immediacy grows even stronger.

7. The word "still" has two meanings. It tells us that the fawn has survived the accident, but also suggests that it is passively awaiting its fate. The line as a whole evokes our pity and sympathy for the creature and we want to resist its conclusion that the fawn will have to die. The reader may even connect the phrase "still-born" to the line, although Stafford doesn't actually use it.

8. The speaker hesitates because the clear plan he had in mind has been thrown into question by his discovery. Instead of just a dead deer, he now has a living fawn to deal with. He may be considering other courses of action. Does he have a pen knife with which he can try to perform a caesarian? Or could he tie the deer to the roof of the car and drive to a vet? Stafford leaves these possibilities out of the poem, but the reader may be thinking of them and weighing the options.

9. Instead of laying out the speaker's thoughts, in stanza four we are given a lot of sensory details. We see the parking lights, hear the engine, and feel the warmth of the exhaust. There are a couple of subtle metaphors going on here. The engine *purring* under the hood may remind us of the fawn inside the doe and the warm exhaust *turning red* suggests the blood of the dead deer lying on the road. These details help to intensify the scene and prepare for the poem's conclusion.

10. "Around our group I could hear the wilderness listen" is the climactic line of the poem. The wilderness, personified, seems to be a god-like force that is overseeing the speaker and judging his actions. The solution to his problem, which seemed obvious at first, has now become much more difficult, and the speaker steps outside of the immediate situation, asking some larger questions about what nature, or fate, or some unnamed force requires of him.

11. "Our group" seems to refer to the specific scene, the doe, the

fawn and the speaker, whereas "us all" is more inclusive. You might think of concentric circles of inclusion, rippling out as the speaker's imagination takes over. There's the local group of the previous line, then there's the wider wilderness around them looking on and listening, and finally the reader of the poem may also be included, as well as humanity as a whole, and the natural world.

12. I've mentioned in my answer to #8 some of the other courses of action that the speaker might have taken. (A pen-knife caesarian, the late-night race to a vet.) But apparently these were not possible for the speaker. He's just an ordinary guy, not a superhero or even an ordinary B-movie hero. We may be disappointed, but the death of the fawn, along with the deer, shows that the speaker has come up against his limits. He does the best he can under the circumstances.

So far we've been talking about the poem in terms of its content, but what about the form? I don't consider the discussion of a poem to be complete until some notice is taken of form, and though in class I might continue asking questions, here let me just offer a couple of observations. "Traveling Through the Dark" is written in four quatrains and a couplet. The form is like a sonnet with an extra quatrain. All of the stanzas are complete in themselves, meaning they are grammatical units ending with a period. It's an orderly arrangement that suggests there is an order behind the world the poem is describing.

If the poem is structured like a sonnet, we might expect to find the end-words rhyming. Well, what about it? William Stafford once wrote that virtually any words can work like rhyme-words, since words sound more like each other than like silence. Looking over these end-words, I hear some echoes but no true rhymes. *Road* and *dead* in the first stanza share a final "d" sound, and *killing* and *belly* in the second stanza have those "ls," and *car* and *cold* share that hard "c" sound. It seems that rather than working in strict rhyme, Stafford is using alliteration to link the end words of the poem. This happens in the third stanza as well, where "reason" matches up with "born" and "waiting" with "hesitated." Not every end-word is linked, but in the fourth stanza we get "engine" and "listen" and in the final couplet "swerving" and "river."

Although most people won't catch these alliterative rhymes on a first reading, they work on us subliminally. They're part of the music of the poem, part of why we feel that the level of speech here is not just talk but has an element of the poetic. The voice in the poem sounds colloquial, but it's slightly elevated, both by the stanza form and the sounds, and that's certainly appropriate to the subject matter. The elevation of the voice fits with the seriousness of the poem's content.

This is a poem about the unexpected difficulties we may encounter in our lives, the spur-of-the-moment decisions we may have to make, the tests we may undergo. With that in mind, notice the poem's title. How casual the first line of the poem seems, but when the phrase is lifted out of context, it takes on a larger significance. Perhaps it's not surprising that this became the title poem of Bill Stafford's National Book Award winning collection.

And one final question: does "Traveling Through the Dark" remind you of some experience you've had—an accident, a shocking encounter—that you might make use of in a poem of your own?

REVISION MEANS SEEING AGAIN

Poets work differently. Some claim to revise hardly at all. They want only the authentic, spontaneous language as it flows from the mind. For me, revision is essential. If I only kept the poems that came spontaneously right the first time, I might write one poem a year—and of the poems I now produce, it wouldn't even be among the best.

I am a hunter and gatherer, and an arranger of language. My desk is covered with books of current poetry and with drafts in various stages of completion. I work there a couple of hours every day, reading, looking out the window, listening to music, waiting for impulse.

WAITING FOR IMPULSE

When impulse comes, it may be that I get some new lines unrelated to the poem or poems I'm then working on; or that impulse may simply be to read over a current draft and scribble on it: change a word here or there, set up a new arrangement of stanzas, cut a passage or move it to another place in the poem. Whatever the impulse, I trust it.

Every working poet knows Ezra Pound's injunction that a poem should contain "absolutely no word that doesn't contribute to the presentation," but in this age of the quickie lyric not many writers are aware of T.S. Eliot's interesting corollary: that a poet's responsibility to the poem is not finished until she/he has said absolutely every word she has to say on the subject. In the clash of these two apparently conflicting rules lies the challenge of revision.

When a draft has been sufficiently modified, I'll save it with a number so that I have my earlier versions to go back to if need be. Sometimes I print out the draft and scribble on it, but usually I just work on the computer. And so it goes, draft following draft. Stale language is dropped and occasionally new material accretes. For, remember, revision means adding as well as subtracting. I add not just new thoughts on the same subject but new subjects. This is the most exciting part: when two apparently unrelated ideas or images come together and make a new whole—that's when I know I really have a poem going.

It may be that I have draft material describing a contemporary Alaskan scene, cross-country skiing, for instance, and then I get something new, for example, an incident from my suburban childhood: how do these two things go together? Well, that's the challenge. It's part of the excitement, I think, part of what Pound was talking about when he spoke of poetry as involving juxtaposition, what Robert Bly means when he insists that poetry must make leaps from one area of consciousness to another.

AT SEA

And the revision continues. All that I've described so far has probably resulted in only a third or fourth draft. I know that usually before a poem is finished I will have at least twenty drafts. I must continue to add, subtract, and rearrange.

I try different length stanzas. Sometimes I count syllables. I'm at sea. The whole thing is in a state of flux. For me, this is the process, and I have to trust it. After all, this is what really interests me. When the poem is finished, I may read it over once in a while, but unless I see new revisions to make I will quickly put it aside. The finished poem ceases to be a focus of my energy.

So now I have six or seven drafts of a poem that began with some Alaskan scene to which I added an incident from my childhood. What now? Perhaps I'm stalled. I don't see where to go with it. What should I do? Why, write some more.

Maybe I've had a dream recently that I can make use of. Or perhaps somewhere in my stack of poem fragments I can find an image or a series of two or three decent lines that can somehow be fit in. There are no rules for this. As Frank O'Hara said, "You just go on your nerve."

The struggle continues for days, for weeks. Sure, sometimes I've stayed up all night with a poem and greeted the dawn with a final version, but what I'm describing here is much more common. I expect normally to spend a couple of hours a day for two to four weeks getting to a final draft; and even then that draft is only provisional. A month, or six months later, I may find the poem in need of further work.

Maybe only a little touching up. Or maybe what I thought was a finished poem will fall apart in my hands. If that happens the poem must go back into the pot of fragments and drafts to be dismembered and reused in other poems.

THE LONG HAUL

In some cases I can trace ideas and images from recent poems back over years and years of drafts and stages. For example, I have a poem about falling off a cliff. Now, it so happens that when I was fifteen I did fall off a cliff. I was unconscious for three days and woke up in a Catholic hospital with a Crucifix on the wall of my room. I had been off in New Mexico on a camping trip. To wake up in that immaculate white room with bloody Christ looking down on me was pretty disorienting.

I have a poem about this which goes back in five utterly different versions to my undergraduate days in college. The first attempt transformed the situation into a plane crash. The crash took place in Juneau, Alaska. At the time I had never been to Alaska and didn't know how dangerous the Juneau airport, girdled by mountains, can be. In any case, the poem itself is quite awful.

In graduate school I wrote a poem about falling down a well. No mention of cliffs or New Mexico, but it was that adolescent experience that I was trying to get at. I had hopes for this version, but somehow it never quite came off. A few years later, I wrote another poem called "The Hole" about—you guessed it—falling down a hole. It was a prose poem, flat and too jokey, but it contained the germ—several key images survived into later versions.

Now, like the two earlier poems—the plane crash and the well-falling—"The Hole" had been brought through many drafts to what I thought was completion. Four years later, however, finding the original unsatisfactory, I rewrote it. I put it into lines and stanzas, shortened it, and cut out some of the jokiness. (The stock market metaphor had to go.) It was still about falling down a hole, but I added a brief note at the beginning about how I had once fallen off a cliff. The connection between that note and the rest of the poem was tenuous, but I thought it might give a stronger grounding in reality to a poem that seemed a bit too disembodied.

A few years later, still dissatisfied, I re-wrote the poem again. I kept a lot of the imagery from the earlier versions about falling down a hole, but now for the first time I managed to work in the actual incident: how I had fallen off a cliff, been unconscious for three days, and woke up in a hospital room with a Crucifix on the wall.

Why? How many times have I heard a beginning writer insist, "That's the way it really happened"? A lame excuse for a poor piece of work. But in my own case, clearly there was the same motive: four different times I had tried to imagine an event that could substitute for the experience I'd actually had. But each time some of the drama had been lost. Since I'm not opposed to altering reality for the sake of artistic truth I suppose I must argue that this poem is an exception: here at least reality exceeded anything my imagination could come up with.

Is that the end of it? Well, I can't be sure. At the Fine Arts Work Center in Provincetown I took some advice from the poet Alan Dugan and dropped a couple of lines. Now I think it's done, but I've been wrong before.

THE ENDLESS FALL: EL MORRO, 1958

Stuck on a sandstone ledge
where—god knows—I should never
have been, I remember starting
to slip. For three days lost
to my body, I sank toward the
bottom of a pool where gray shapes
splashed around me near the center
of a fierce design. Deeper down
the pool became a room:

did the mind exude the eerie
soft blue flame by which
the walls could be read,
here a bone, a shell, there
an odd repeating element
like the sun. Meanwhile my body
lay—skull cracked, face crusted,
front teeth gone, male nurses
adjusting the needles taped

to my veins—unconscious away
where Christ's bloody effigy sagged
on St. Joseph's wall. And as the last
light started to vacate that hole
I met another self, there at the
center: he drifted under my skin,
breathed through my lungs and dreamed
himself into my wounds. Like brother
assassins, meeting and parting,

we float in this vacuum forever.

THE HUMP

The process of revision as I've been describing it may seem itself to be endless. In fact, though, as I work on a poem I find that I am discovering and then clarifying the subject. "The Endless Fall" took so long because I seemed to resist the poem's true material, or perhaps because when I began I wasn't ready to face it.

Resistance is part of the process of discovery, and usually somewhere around the fifteenth draft I reach a point where my frustration at not being able to get it right peaks. Not infrequently I am tempted to abandon the poem—and sometimes I do—but more often the resistance is actually a good sign. There's a psychological barrier here, a hump I have to get over: something in the lumpy potential of the material that strikes deep and that I must work through.

Commonly, this is where I make the last new additions to the poem. I will often throw out chunks and shift lines and stanzas wildly about. My frustration has given me renewed energy, and, careless of consequences, I attack the poem and try to master it.

When I'm through with this key draft or series of drafts, there is a sense of having made it over the top: I can see that the poem is pretty close to finished. I must still push the lines around, find the right stanzas, and order the material, but this—to shift metaphors—is a mopping up operation. Now, like a print in developer, the poem comes clearer and clearer with each draft. At last I can begin to see what it's all been about.

The Click

And then there's a subtle 'click' and the poem is finished. I never can be sure which draft will do it, but, no matter, if I've been an honest craftsman, eventually the 'click' will come.

The Final Cut

And is that all? Sometimes it is. But there's often one more stage. After I've done all I can with a poem and it seems finished, I must put it aside for a week, a month, or even six months—and then come back to it with a fresh eye. This is when it helps to show the poem to my writer friends and get their comments and suggestions. This stage is comparable to the test screenings movie-makers give their films before the final cut. Up to now, while the material was still in flux, comments from others would most likely have interfered. After all, I hadn't yet discovered what the poem was about for myself; and if I didn't know, how could anyone else?

But now I think I do know. The poem is clear, at least to me; I've heard that 'click.' Now I need to check out my intuition. Do others see what I've been up to? Where have I succeeded, where failed? The comments need not be elaborate, though sometimes a full critique will help. Often a single sentence (often containing the word 'slack') is enough to send me back through the poem cutting and slashing. For now I'm ready with the knife and it's a common failing, even after all these drafts, that the poem is still looser than it has to be. The material I cut away (a couple of lines, a stanza) will not be missed. Reading the poem over in a day or two, I will find it hard to imagine how it was ever any longer. Now it's finished.

What's it All About, Alfie?

For me, and I suspect for many other poets, the revision of individual poems is part of a larger enterprise. It is one aspect of defining one's aesthetics. The problem is to see clearly the limitations of your work so far, and to attempt to remedy its failings in the poems still to be written. And, seen in this light, I can't fully conceal from myself the suspicion that what I am ultimately revising is myself.

49 WRITERS INTERVIEW WITH JOHN MORGAN

– *Spear-Fishing on the Chatanika* –

INTERVIEW BY DEB VANASSE

How did you decide which poems to gather in this collection?
When Jessie Lendennie asked if I had a book to submit to Salmon, I said do you want to see the long version or the short one? She said the long version. That was the "new and selected poems." Choosing poems was pretty intuitive. I wanted a balance between new and old and I wanted to give each of my earlier books roughly equal space. Essentially, I just went through and picked the poems I felt were the strongest, the ones I tend to include in readings. There were a couple of surprises in the new section, poems that I'd published in magazines but had forgotten about.

How did you settle on the book title Spear-Fishing on the Chatanika, *echoing the poem title "Scouts Spear-Fishing on the Chatanika"?*
I wanted a title that made a connection to Alaska and that had an element of drama. That poem is a war poem, reflecting back on Vietnam, and also a father and son poem, and both of those themes run through the book.

There's so much to savor in this book. Let's start with poems gathered in groups: "Cape Prince of Wales Alaska: a Suite"; "Six Poems from Above the Tanana"; and "Spells and Auguries." Tell us about your process of creating poems in groups. Do you set out with that intention, or do you discover the collective energy over time?

Each sequence came about differently. "Cape Prince of Wales: A Suite" came from a notebook I kept during a three day visit to the village of Wales at the tip of the Seward Peninsula. I modeled it on some poems written in numbered free verse sections by John Logan and I knew roughly what it would look like from the start. The poems in "Above the Tanana" are all set at the same location, a ledge overlooking the river with a long view south to the Alaska Range. I wrote one per month for a year, and when I'd written two or three of them I realized what form the sequence would take. Since then I've continued to write poems set at that spot which aren't officially part of the sequence. "Spells and Auguries" took longer to work out. When my son Ben went into the hospital in a coma, I tried to write about it but it was mainly for my own sanity, to keep a grip on who I was. He was in the coma for five days and it changed him quite a bit and changed our lives. I thought I might write a memoir about the experience and went back to the original poems to see what I could draw from them. As I suspected, they weren't very good, but they brought the experience back to me and instead of a memoir I wrote a sequence of 24 sonnets.

Among your new poems, "Poet Charged in Scrape" is one of my favorites. In it, you turn unfortunate Daniel Poet's mishap ("The Coast Guard charged Poet with negligence in the accident," says AP) into a remarkable poem, from "the moon was low and each ripple had tiny sickles darting its peak" to "only a little meaning spilled through the crack in the hull." When did you know this news snippet had to be a poem, and how did it come together?

As soon as I saw the article in the News-Miner, with a guy actually named "Poet" screwing up and causing the accident, I figured there was a poem in it. I kept the subject in my head for a week or so and when I sat down to write it, it came pretty easily. It's playful and lyrical in contrast to some of the darker poems in the collection.

In the new poem "Kindling: For Ben," you've written yet another powerful piece generated from the long-term consequences of your son's childhood illness, a poem that builds on the collection in "Spells and Auguries." How important is it for poets to probe painful and personal experiences?

"Kindling: for Ben" describes a grand mal seizure and I wrote it because I feel writers need to face their experiences head-on, no matter how painful.... You confront it and then, through the writing, you manage to get some control over it. In this case, though, the control is only at the margin. There's a breakdown of form in the middle of the poem as the horror of the seizure takes over, and then at the end the form creeps back in in the last couple of stanzas. It's one of the bleakest poems in the book and I wondered about including it, but I feel the poem that follows, "An Easy Dayhike, Mt. Rainier," which views Ben's seizures in a more accepting way, helps to redeem it.

AN INTERVIEW WITH JOHN MORGAN

Permafrost, Vol. 32 (Summer, 2010)

[Poetry staff members Airika Parker and Cody Kucker
interviewed John in April 2010.]

PERMAFROST: *What is the process of selecting poems for this kind of
collection? How much control did you have over which poems would be
included?*

JOHN MORGAN: It can vary. In this case the publisher (Jessie
Lendennie, Salmon Poetry) asked me to send a manuscript. A year
went by, I had almost forgotten. Then she emailed me and said she
wanted to do it. She had no suggestions; she simply took the
manuscript. I made a few editing changes when it was in the
process of getting ready to go to press, but they were very small.

P: *What are the concerns of putting this type of collection together in terms
of the overall narrative, speaker, tone and voice?*

JM: The process of selecting the poems was, essentially, to find a
balance from my three earlier books and new poems. Roughly, half
the book is new. The process of selecting was intuitive, simply
'these poems I like.' I trusted the voice is consistent enough that it
isn't going to be jarring. What I found in putting it together is that
my style had changed. I guess I knew it at the time – that I was
changing – but it sort of faded into the past. Looking at the earlier
poems in the book, they have a more romantic feel. They tend to
be in fairly long lines. Theodore Roethke was an influence. There
is a move toward irony in some of the later poems, not that it was
ever absent but it is more highlighted, and different kinds of line

breaks come into the poems. Reading William Carlos Williams had an effect on my lines. The new sections cover a long period of time, about twenty years. I was choosing from a larger group of poems and making selections.

P: *Was there anything that surprised you about looking at those old poems, about the poet you were or the poems you had written?*
JM: Well, they seemed like a young man's poems, [laughs] some of them. I am happy with them, but they aren't the kinds of poems I write today, for better or worse.

P: *The earlier speaker was more romantic, the forms are a little looser than when you get into "Spells and Auguries," or even the selections from* Walking Past Midnight *and you mentioned irony playing a greater role. Why is "Scouts Spear-Fishing on the Chatanika" the title poem for this collection? Does it speak to who you've become as a poet?*
JM: It does seem to embody some of the larger themes in the book. There are quite a few war poems. I was never in the war, but Vietnam was certainly a disaster that happened to all of us at the time. I was actually born during World War II; some of my earliest memories are of bombers flying overhead. The element of irony, the main irony in that poem, is the child's point of view and the adult's point of view and how they clash.

P: *Poems like "A Man Without Legs" and "The Siege of Leningrad" veer from the consistent voice of the speaker that runs through most of this collection. Did you find that using another voice and subject was helpful, particularly in the war poems?*
JM: The Leningrad poem came out of a book I read, *The 900 Days* by Harrison Salisbury, which quoted from diaries that had been preserved that recorded the suffering of the people including one by a teenage girl. It seemed appropriate to give it to the girl to speak rather than trying to take on that kind of experience with my own voice.

P: *The idea of place comes up in this collection in many different ways. Alaska is explicitly mentioned throughout the text. What role does Alaska play and how does the landscape help to facilitate the merging of external and internal conflict?*

JM: Alaska is a major influence on the poems. There are quite a few poems that are set in one specific location, overlooking the Tanana River. It is simply where I go to sit and wait for a poem. There's always some sensory information there as my inner thoughts go in various directions, so it's the perfect scene to try to incorporate the internal and the external.

P: *You do that beautifully in those poems.*
JM: Thank you. I think that's the central voice of the book, even though I don't start with it. As the book evolves that's where I come through most directly.

P: *How does the Alaskan lifestyle stand up to things that need to be contained in modern poetry to stay contemporary?*
JM: At one point I sent the manuscript to an editor in New York who wrote back to say 'there is way too much Alaska in this book. People in New York don't know Alaska.' [smiles] That was before Sarah Palin I guess. I'm a New Yorker. That's where I grew up. The move to Alaska was unexpected. It is a remarkable place. It has certainly been an important part of my own development and that's why it's in the poetry.

P: *You recently had the chance to be the Poet in Residence at Denali National Park. How did that experience differ from the time you frequently spend on the Tanana?*
JM: I was living in a cabin in the park and I was completely free to do whatever I felt like doing. Everyday I felt like I was having new and unexpected experiences. There were eagles all over. There was a fox den nearby. There was a field with over a hundred caribou in it. It had a real impact on me. I had a sense that I was in a different relationship to nature than I had been before. I'm not conventionally religious—but it came close to being a religious experience.

P: *I know that as a Poet in Residence you're required to produce a poem for the park to use. Does the process differ when you have a poem that needs to be written as opposed to working with something that arises naturally?*
JM: Yes, I think you're right to point out the difference. The things that had an impact on me, that I chose to write about, were not the standard kind of nature poems. I only wrote about the things

that I felt 'well this is really new and interesting and I better write about it' [laughs]. Hopefully that overcomes the problem.

P: *Being from New York, do you find Alaska more suitable for your sensibilities? Do you find yourself writing urban poems in other places?*
JM: When I came up here I thought, 'gee, I am a newbie. I better not write about Alaska for a while. I better just absorb it.' That resolution lasted for about a week, and then I started writing about Alaska because there is so much here. It has such an impact. The first poem in the book is set in the Caribbean; it's a diving poem. I put it first to say, 'just because I am an Alaskan doesn't mean I always write about Alaska.' It also seemed like a way in to the collection. Diving has a mythic element to it that is comparable to going into a book of poetry. You're going to see some new things, and you need instruction on how to read a book of poetry. It's kind of an instruction poem.

P: *The idea of the 'Alaskan Poet' seems to be a hot topic right now. Do you have a take on it?*
JM: There doesn't seem to be any reason to shy away from writing about Alaska. If you are in New York and writing about New York City you have Frank O'Hara to worry about, Walt Whitman, Hart Crane. You will not be the first to write about the urban experience. In Alaska there have been important writers too, but Alaska has its own space that is unusual.

P: *You studied under Robert Lowell and refer to him several times throughout the* Selected Poems. *How has Lowell influenced your work?*
JM: He influenced me more as a poet than as a teacher. He was hands-off as a teacher. Poetry for him was a calling, not merely a craft but something that you gave your life to, and that was an important influence. Later, in grad school, is when I started to read his poetry carefully.

P: *Speaking of grad school, you studied at Iowa. What was that like for you?*
JM: Disorienting because of the number of poets that year. Many of them were very talented. I had to learn pretty fast that what I was doing from my undergraduate writing was not going to stand up. I was engaged at the time, to Nancy. She would send me

postcards from the Gardner Museum in Boston. I would write her letters responding to the paintings on the postcards. Those became the first poems that I felt really had my voice and had some craft to them. They were love poems in letter form.

P: *What is the role of form in your work? What are the limitations and liberations that you find in form?*
JM: Our mental world is full of competing material. In a poem you find some aspect of that world that you can get a handle on, and the handle is form. My poems begin, often, with free association, not the very rigorous lines and stanzas that develop as I work through the material and get a feel for the direction it could take.

P: *How did putting "Spells and Auguries" into sonnet form help facilitate the composition of that experience?*
JM: I started writing the sonnets for Ben while he was still in the coma. It was a way of keeping contact with a part of myself that I thought was endangered. The thought that he might die was devastating, so the poems were therapeutic. I used the sonnet form because it gave me a sense of control…. Probably none of the poems really resemble the sonnets I started with, but that was the generative material.

P: *Your family seems central to your work. How do you balance the role of father, son, husband and poet?*
JM: It wasn't something that I expected. I didn't expect to get married until I proposed. I didn't expect to have children, but then a time came that we were ready. Once you have children you have to deal with it [laughs]. Jeff is a poet. Ben is a musician. So those are the values in our family. We're lucky to be able to do those things.

P: *This brings up another question I have: throughout the collection you achieve a wonderful balance of lyric and narrative and are continually able, in Eliot's terms, to turn some very particular experiences into general truths. Do you find yourself being cautious of that, in terms of becoming too personal?*
JM: This comes back to an idea of who the reader of the poems might be. I have an internal dialogue based on my relationship with some friends who read my work. Their reactions become my internalized critic. I have a sense of how they might react, and that

helps me draw lines. I certainly don't begin that way, the poems start with my own impulse.

P: *Was it a long process learning where to draw that line? Have you learned any hard lessons?*

JM: We'll see [laughs]. At the time I was starting to write these very personal poems it wasn't unique because it was the period of confessional poetry in the 60s with Lowell as one of the major figures, Sylvia Plath, Ann Sexton writing about her daughter. What I was doing was not really on the edge compared to some of what those poets wrote. I don't consider my poems confessional. They are personal. They are things I might say to a member of the family. They are not generally things I would conceal within an intimate circle. I like that intimacy as a part of the voice.

P: *It is definitely there, especially in a poem like "Sonnet of the Lost Labor." It is quite stunning and powerful. There is a lot to balance in a poetic voice. What about the balance between music and story?*

JM: The music of the language has to be there. I tend to like poems that have some narrative elements, not necessarily a full story but an element of tension that you get from dramatic situations. The emotional element is the other thing in the poem that has to be there. You need the sound and the feeling.

P: *Something else we appreciated about your work was the humor that ran throughout, poems like "Moo" and "Time off From Bad Behavior." Can you say something about the role humor plays in this collection?*

JM: It's just part of my personality that comes out. I'm glad that I can get it into the poems. I know some very funny people who write only serious poems. It's partly a pacing device. As I put the book together I knew that after a few heavy blows I needed something a little lighter to give the reader a sense of stepping back and hopefully being amused.

P: *It worked. With the completion of this collection you have the opportunity to look back on your journey as a poet. What are your landmark moments?*

JM: The most important thing was getting to the first poems that I thought were good, as good as I could do at the time. Those were the poems for Nancy that I wrote in graduate school my first year. Everything else follows from that. Getting a first book published was important, but that was more of a professional accomplishment than a discovery of voice. This new book is important in a similar way and does have the quality of summarizing my entire career.

P: *What advice do you have for new poets in terms of becoming the type of poet they want to be?*
JM: Write on a regular basis. A lot of the poems I now value I dragged out of myself over a blank computer screen, just to get them started. Not that they were necessarily promising from the start, but I stayed with it and found where the material could go. That is my process. It is an amazing life—to produce over a long period of time and then see the result. The other thing is to read. Read widely.

P: *It must be a very proud moment to have this collection coming out.*
JM: Yes.

P: *Thank you for your time John. It has been a pleasure.*
JM: Thank *you.*

IV.
A POET IN HIS PLACE

LETTER FROM FAIRBANKS
(1976-77)

The leaves on the aspen and birch trees have already yellowed, many have fallen. It's mid-September as I write, and within a week the trees will be bare. By October 1st, snow is expected, and after that winter will be with us till the end of April. Long-term residents tell us it's not the cold or even the dark, but the length of the winter that gets people down. "Cabin fever" is the name of the syndrome. It breaks up marriages and is a contributing factor to the homicide rate here, one of the highest in the nation.

The frontier atmosphere is relished and exaggerated, and relatively large modern structures like the new Teamster clinic and recreation hall get their log cabin facades. The Teamsters are here, as everyone knows, for the pipeline. Fairbanks, the most northerly city of its size (50,000) in the country, is the administrative and supply center for pipeline construction. Workers on leave from their camps along the route come here to blow their pay on liquor and women and gambling, just as panners did in the old gold-mining days. Gold built this town in the first place, and now that pipeline construction's beginning to slacken off, local boosters are looking ahead to the gasline that will inevitably follow, for there is gas in Prudhoe Bay as well as oil. The route of the gasline is up for grabs, and if it goes through Canada, as now seems likely, Fairbanks, dependent as it has always been on the wealth of the earth, may not have much of a future.

But for now the pipeline boom is still on. The mystique of the pipeline has certainly been felt outside, but it's strongest here in Alaska, where a doctor working in the Teamster clinic prefers to say, without embellishment, that he works "on the pipeline." And one wonders if the *News-Miner* isn't exaggerating just a bit in its daily stories of murders, muggings, and police raids on gambling houses and houses of prostitution. Just yesterday, Governor Jay Hammond (who has the physique of a woodsman and wears a woodsman's beard) announced a "crisis in law enforcement" and volunteered the use of state troopers to patrol the streets. The city fathers thanked the governor but felt such extraordinary measures were not necessary.

If, as an early morning stroll down Second Avenue will reveal, drunkenness is a problem, the City Council has a measure before it that would help. There are currently no restrictions at all on bar hours. The new law would close them at 2 a.m. Opposition from tavern owners has been fierce.

Yet this is all part of the mystique, and it would be wrong to imply that a rough frontier atmosphere dominates the town. The governor wouldn't have come at all except that Fairbanks is the second largest population center in the state. By daylight the downtown area, with a Penney's, a Woolworth's, a Sears "catalog center," its streets recently re-directed one-way to accommodate increasing traffic, resembles any number of nondescript Midwestern American towns. For it is the Midwest, rather than the West Coast or Canada, which Fairbanks under this unusually sunny fall most closely resembles. There are more churches here than bars, and if an Ozark twang is often heard among those associated with the pipeline, the accent most common among the more permanent residents is Midwestern.

In 1940, the population was about twelve thousand. Most of those have now moved out or died, and you rarely run into anyone who was actually born here. A typical resident may come from small-town Iowa, or the Dakotas, and local speech reflects this derivation. "Have a nice day," the lady behind the counter in Penney's will tell you even at four in the afternoon with the day mostly gone. "Have a nice day," says the serviceman at a local Texaco as you pull away from the pump.

But nothing in Iowa or the Dakotas resembles the stunning white-capped peaks of the Alaska Range, rising on clear days like a marvelous mirage to the south. Mt. McKinley, a hundred and fifty miles away, reaches 20,000 feet higher than the flat Tanana Valley in which Fairbanks lies. And of course nothing in the "lower forty-eight" matches the spectacular auroral displays which even in August this year filled the night sky with pulsating beacons of green and white.

Nor does even a Dakota winter match the 60 and 70 below temperatures we can expect here. Preparations have already begun. Cars must be "winterized," which in addition to changing to an extremely light oil means the installation of a "circulating heater." Operating off electric current, these devices keep the engine fifty degrees or so warmer than the outside air while the car sits overnight. Lots around town include a "plug-in" attached to each meter. A car left standing just two or three hours at fifty below and without the heater would be unlikely to start.

Of course we worry about ourselves as well as our car. Warm parkas, down mittens, and 'Sorrel' boots with replaceable felt liners will be needed. Those liners help ward off the dampness which contributes to frostbite. As soon as you get inside, we're told, take your liners out and put them next to the electric heater to dry.

Now the fall air is crisply clear, but by mid-winter (reflecting the fragile ecology of such a northerly location) ice-fog will be upon us. In the windless conditions which prevail here at extremely low temperatures all the water vapor in the air (fed by car exhausts) freezes and sits, held down in a temperature inversion by an even colder layer of arctic air above. Added to the twenty-hour nights, the ice fog reduces visibility to a matter of feet. On icy roads in the fog, accidents are the rule. No wonder many insurers are quitting the area.

"No studded snowtires allowed before September 15," says the sign as we start our drive up the Steese Highway. Eleven miles north, the Elliot Highway branches off, and here the pipeline begins. Sections of pipe are stacked not far from the road, and the long serpentine belly—more impressive in this wide hilly landscape than one had expected—moves off toward Deadhorse and Prudhoe Bay. It seems alien here because it is so completely modern, so rigid and purposeful as it lies on this spruce-covered land. At peak construction, the pipeline employed some 21,000 workers, but the number is smaller than that now, and when completed it will require fewer than five hundred to monitor and maintain it—or so say its sponsors, assuming no doubt that the welds hold.

Ten miles further along, having diverged from the pipeline, we come to Cleary Summit (2,233 feet), from which McKinley is dimly visible. Fairbanks, in its valley, has sunk from view, and now the vastness of this state becomes apparent. Only an occasional radar installation or ski lodge out here. Mostly just miles of spruce, aspen, and birch. After a while the highway is a wide single lane of dirt.

We come to an "Historical Marker," pull off the road, and have lunch. A thick section of rusted pipe calls back an earlier period of boom. In the Twenties, a large-scale construction effort produced the Davidson Ditch and Pipeline through which over three million gallons of water an hour were diverted to gold mining dredges forty miles away. At that time millions and millions of dollars in gold were pumped out of the land.

Farther on there are occasional campgrounds, and highway crews wet down the road which has suffered in the current drought. We are heading toward the Yukon River (though we won't make it that far on this trip), and only northern Maine in our experience resembles this wooded vacancy.

Gradually trees give way to a hilly tundra. Wayside parking areas mark hiking trails. Sixty-six miles out, Miracle Mile Roadhouse is the farthest north access point to the Chatanika River canoe trail. The Chatanika is a class 2 (medium difficult) stream. Canoeists are warned to watch for low overhanging trees, log jams, and fast white water. For these risks they may be rewarded with the sight of a moose, come down to the stream to drink.

Up at Eagle Summit—five hours out of town and as far as we can go if we're to get back by nightfall—we scan the tundra for migrating caribou, but don't see any. With the vegetation already turning, the reddish-brown hills stretch like a carpet for many miles in all directions. People come here on June 21, to watch the sun fail to set at midnight. The tundra is spongy underfoot. At 3600 feet the air is cool even in late August, and the distances covered by the eye are vast. Far to the north—more miles than we can quite grasp—lies the shadowy Brooks Range, visible on clear days—or so a sign claims. What we see are probably some intervening hills. To see the Brooks Range from here would be like standing on top of the World Trade Center and seeing on the horizon the Washington Monument. That's the scale of things in Alaska.

&

We'd received many warnings about mosquitoes which swarm up from the bogs when the snow melts in spring, but I'm happy to report that by mid-August when we got here, the worst of the season was past.

&

Whenever Anchorage comes into the conversation around here, you can be pretty sure that the likelihood of another earthquake which, like the one in 1964, will utterly decimate that (warmer, larger) city will be raised.

&

Item: a creative writing teacher at the university leaves his job in order to work on the pipeline: he can earn enough in six months to support himself, his wife, and two kids for the rest of the year while he writes his novel.

&

On the edge of town there is a musk ox farm run by the university. These exotic bovines are being raised for their wonderfully soft and warm fur which the Eskimos turn into wool for scarves and blankets. The wool is called "qiviut."

&

There is a constant turnover in the population here. Newcomers are frequently stopped on the street and asked directions by other newcomers. Every weekend at numerous garage sales, those leaving pass along their worldly possessions to those who have just arrived. Certainly it takes a special temperament to settle in for the long haul, but there are those who see the merits of living in a place where, only ten miles out, one can acquire land very reasonably and build a home with no neighbors in sight. Such people will tell you that properly dressed you can be warmer here than in parts of the "lower forty-eight," because when the temperature drops to fifty below there's never any wind. The ice-fog, of course, never reaches beyond the edge of town. And fluctuations give occasional days in mid-winter when the temperature rises as high as ten or twenty above— perfect for cross-country skiing and snow-mobiling, fine for hiking or just pottering around the yard.

Of course in winter daylight is limited. There may be as little as three hours of it. But, say the true settlers, those gorgeous moon- and aurora-lit days are the best, when the white earth seems to give back more light than it received from the dark sky and you live in a world made up more of spirit than matter. Ghostly, unreal, and marvelously cold.

Newcomers may be skeptical. Paul Salter has just taken over as Dean of the College of Arts and Sciences at the Fairbanks branch of the University of Alaska. An urban geographer, he comes here from an entirely different climate, having been an assistant dean at the University of Miami. When he flew up in June to be interviewed, he had to switch planes in Chicago, and as he tells it, a rather sullen-looking young man got on with him at O'Hare and took a seat just in front. As the plane was taxiing out to the runway, the young man jumped up and cried, "No, I can't do it! I can't go back!" The plane turned around and returned to the gate. A pipe fitter, the young man had spent the past two years working on the line.

Tomorrow, September 18, beginning at 8 a.m., the Equinox Marathon will take place. The 135 entrants will start out at Patty Field and proceed uphill for thirteen miles to the top of Ester Dome, an altitude gain of two thousand feet, then return to the field. Only the Pike's Peak run is considered tougher. We are losing sunlight now at a rate of seven minutes per day. In a few weeks the rivers will freeze up and the ground will be covered with snow. From then on it will be uphill into late March or April, when the winter finally turns around.

～

A JANUARY POSTSCRIPT:

As the days shortened down to a couple of hours around the middle of December, even at noon the sun lay barely above the horizon. It would rise to the southeast at about ten in the morning and struggle along the top of the southern mountains for a few hours, setting by one-thirty in the afternoon. We missed the full brilliance of day, living instead through extended dawns which merged into long beautiful sunsets. It was important to make the effort to get outside during those few hours, otherwise we'd lose the day entirely.

Now, in mid-January, the sun is making its return. In one way we've been lucky. While parts of the "lower forty-eight" were having one of the severest winters on record, ours has been mild. The first week in January saw temperatures rise into the thirties. One day a record high of forty degrees was registered. And though we've had occasional lows of twenty or thirty below, we've missed so far those promised weeks of minus fifty, minus sixty, minus seventy, without which we can hardly be said to have experienced a Fairbanks winter.

Not that we're complaining.

But, as in other parts of the country, the winter has been light on snow. Skiers are unhappy, and so are the "mushers." This is the season for dogsled races, but several meets have had to be cancelled due to the sparseness of snow-cover. Boulders and logs normally deeply buried at this time of year are lying exposed, dangerous obstacles for high-speed sledders.

Four inches of snow fell last week, though, and that gave the more daring racers a margin they felt safe with. In the fifteen degree warmth a large crowd gathers at the Alaskan Mushers Association racing grounds on Farmers Loop Road, north of town. Just the other day a car slammed into a moose near here— or that's the rumor we've heard. The dogs seem even more eager than their masters to get out on the ten mile course. They strain in their harnesses and some leap straight up in the air to burn off their uncontrollable energy while the starter counts down the last few seconds and half a dozen people holding back the sled struggle against the pull of the dogs so they won't leave the starting post early. And then on "Go!" instantly the twelve dogs spring smoothly forward, the musher behind her sled on the runners, her post number pinned in large green numerals to the back of her parka. Within a matter of seconds they're starting to make a wide curve at the far end of the field. With distance they shrink to a dark silhouette—the dogs in pairs, the sled and musher—against the snow. Soon they disappear into the woods.

Racing against time ("electronically clocked"), a new sled starts out from the post every two minutes. The dogs, bred for speed, are much smaller and sleeker than the usual husky, though occasionally a larger dog—looking like a sheep among wolves—will have made the team. Women compete with men as mushers, and local businesses sponsor individual competitors who have the expense of raising and training as many as seventy or eighty dogs. The dogs are not pets by any means. They're penned outside through the cold winters, lest they go soft and lose the competitive edge.

And now, thirty minutes later, with sleds still starting off at two minute intervals, the voice on the loud speaker directs our attention to the edge of the woods, where the first of the returning teams has just emerged, dogs still straining forward, the musher directing them with oral commands to which they respond as readily as well trained horses to a rein. Tongues flapping at the sides of their mouths, they cross the finish line smoothly and with little noticeable slackening of pace from their opening burst. The first sled to come in is timed at thirty-five minutes, thirty-four hundredths of a minute. The second sled covered the ten miles more quickly by half a minute and brings in what will prove to be the best time of the day. As we start for home, the sun, which had been a yellow spotlight glaring out of the southern sky, has paled and softened, and the clouds to the southwest are tinted orange.

Almost half a year in Alaska. We've eaten moose roast and caribou stew. A few weeks ago we were wakened out of sleep by a small earthquake. It came through like a shockwave, rattling everything in the apartment and even the building itself, but causing no damage.

That same week we saw the most spectacular display of

Northern Lights since our arrival. We noticed it as we came out of a restaurant after dinner: at first several thick ropes of light looping around the sky. We'd seen that kind of thing before, but tonight it was going on all over the sky—not just one or two strands of light but many. One main loop circled back on itself and broke in half, and these in turn lengthened and snaked across the sky. It's this restlessness, the constant looping and shifting, that one is least prepared for. As we watched, one of the strands of light began to shimmer. It dropped closer to the earth and took on a veil-like transparency, a radiant curtain of light with folds of pale pink, white, and metallic green. A few minutes later the aurora had receded deep into the sky and stood almost motionless, branching like a vast tree against a vaster backdrop of stars. The cold was beginning to get to us now, and we went inside, but hours later the Northern Lights were still active in the sky.

LETTER FROM WALES, ALASKA
(1977)

Here at the tip of the Seward Peninsula, where it points west into the Bering Strait, an arrow on the shack that stands as the village post office also points west.

Neatly hand-lettered it announces: "Russia, 30 Miles."

Partly to verify this fact, the other day I climbed the steep ridge along the single dirt street that constitutes the Eskimo village of Wales, Alaska (pop. 130). It was a warm day, near fifty, sunny, and the wind which usually blows in a confusing, gusty, shifting fashion was temporarily calm. I followed the small stream that provides summer water for the village up to its source in a tundra spring. Snow buntings flitted around me, individually curious but cautious in groups, each warning the others not to get too close. Among the dark gray rocks I caught a fleeting glimpse of a bulky arctic hare. Two hours out of town, climbing toward the bright sun, as I neared the ridge-line there appeared on a farther ridge a large silver dish, rivaling the sun: an Air Force radar station, staring west.

I sat down on a boulder and turned that way myself. The village had disappeared below, and I looked out on the Bering Sea. To the north, more water: Kotzebue Sound and the Chukchi Sea. Mid-water, on this unusually clear morning lay the two Diomedes: islands separated by less than three miles, yet one full day apart. Little Diomede, part of Alaska and the U.S., is situated on our side of the International Date Line. Big Diomede, against which the smaller island is a dark silhouette, lies on the far side of the line, a day ahead of us. It belongs to the U.S.S.R.

Still farther off, about fifty-five miles from where I sat, I could see through haze the dim outline of the Siberian Coast.

I was, in effect, looking through time, into tomorrow, looking ahead by exactly one day, and I was somewhat reassured that the far coast appeared innocent, peaceful, reassured though I knew there would be large silver dishes out there staring back over here at us; and beyond the radar stations, missiles too, much like our own. But from the unusual vantage point I had, it was as easy to look back as ahead. For, if archaeologists are correct, the spot where I was sitting, sipping a six ounce can of Dole's unsweetened pineapple juice ($.57 at the Wales Native Store)*, looked out on the route of crossing of the first people ever to set foot in the New World. And not just men had crossed here, but mastodons, mammoths, the hairy rhino: here lay the landbridge, here the crossings wave upon wave, Siberians moving east, animals first, then man. Indians, Eskimos.

In addition to its Eskimos, Wales is home to a handful of Caucasians and a Filipino-American couple who manage the naval weather station. Most of the Eskimos are out of town now, gone "camping" thirty miles to the northeast, where, at camp, they follow traditional ways: hunting, fishing, gathering berries. Those currently in town seem to wish they weren't—they feel the pull of the camp—but they're here usually out of a sense of responsibility to their children: school started this week. The kids having a good time out at camp will be falling behind in their schoolwork. Talking the other evening to my host, Walter Weyapuk, I could sense his hopes for his daughter Leah. A high school graduate himself (as is his wife, though this is not at all common in Wales), he patiently coached the bright, round-faced, smiling girl with her math and writing.

Walter is the postmaster (Wales, AK 99783). Compact, with a black wispy beard, black moustache, he smokes as he talks, his hair shoulder-length like mine, a digital watch on his wrist. There's a mound behind the village, he tells me, a designated "Historical Site." Another village once stood there, its people in friendly competition with the people of Wales. But as time went on, feuding developed, fighting maybe; anyway, the ones over there picked up and moved. They went up north to the village of Point Hope. When Walter Weyapuk left Wales to attend high school, his roommate came from Point Hope. They compared notes and found that the two village traditions agree on this point.

* For today's equivalent price, multiply by 4.

The Weyapuks, Walter, his wife Flo, Leah, and an adopted two-year-old son, much-loved Michael, occupy a three bedroom prefab house provided by the Bureau of Indian Affairs. Now, Eskimos aren't Indians, but at $35 a month, they'll take the house. Many other families in town have identical dwellings, and those who don't usually live worse. This place is comfortable, even if it isn't quite secure against the arctic winds. Its kitchen—a common feature in the village—has two stoves and no refrigerator (the enclosed front porch serves well enough for that). Two stoves because, should the village generator conk out, a back-up heat source will be needed.

Yes, there's electricity, but no plumbing. The BIA-provided bathtub serves for storage. I noticed that it currently contains a basket filled with dirty laundry, two larges bags of Friskies Dog Dinner, several rolls of paper towels, a rusted two gallon can, cables, some boxes of Pampers, a rug, and a fancy oval Cardin make-up box. For a toilet, the now-traditional "honey pot"—a covered plastic bucket with a toilet seat above a disposable plastic bag.

I've felt a lot of different things in the three days since I flew in from Nome. The plane that brought me, a rickety six-seater provided by Forster Air Charter, followed the coastline for the last half hour no more than 100 feet off the water. Along the way we saw five or six dead walruses on the beach, and each time my pilot moved in closer, hoping to spot one with tusks. No luck—they'd already been removed. I'll admit I was scared as we banked steeply around those rocky points of land that jut out into the sea—scared but exhilarated. And I was feeling something else, something more disturbing—separation anxiety, I decided it was. It was like being sent away to camp for the first time.

In Nome I was told it would be rough, that I would see some disturbing things, some things that would disgust me. I haven't found it that way. Look, I'm from New York: what could be rougher than that? Still, my moods here fluctuate, intense interest giving way to periods of intense boredom. The thought of living here—no movie house, no TV for God's sake!—horrifies me at times. At other moments it seems perfectly natural. The Weyapuks' extended family—the grandmother (a distinguished village elder), the many uncles and cousins—takes in a good percentage of the population here, and reminds me in some ways of my own large New York Jewish family, with similar tensions, intimacies, rewards.

In many ways Wales is much less cut-off than I'd expected. Radio, telephone, mail service, CB, hi-fi all connect it to the fast-moving world out there. "I collect albums," Walter tells me. "I can pick up the phone, call Anchorage, and have the records I want in five days." His latest shipment just came in: Linda Ronstadt, Billy Joel, the Stones ("Emotional Rescue"), Eagles, Lipps Inc. "The Greeks Don't Like No Freaks" gloats the hi-fi, as we sip tea, munch on pizza, thumb through *Newsweek*, a Sears catalog, the *National Enquirer*. All these reach Wales, and more.

And yet it's not the same. Walter tells me about the spring hunt. First whales (beluga and bowhead), then bearded seals, then walrus, each for a period of weeks coming up the coast on their annual migrations. This spring—much excitement—for the first time in ten years the village got a bowhead, a small one, thirty-five feet. When that happens, everybody in the village gets some, everybody eats better. With chicken at the village store going for $7.50 apiece, subsistence hunting is no joke.

Still, the Weyapuks do vary their diet with an occasional chicken, beef (generally cooked as soup), with pizza (the Chef Boyardee pepperoni mix costs $3.02, but if you live here you get used to the prices). My first meal in town was bearded seal with onions. For dessert, "Eskimo ice-cream": reindeer fat and sugar whipped up over salmon berries crisp and sweet. I enjoyed the seal, went easy on the ice-cream.

The other day Eric flew in. Tall, bearded, white, a man of the Sixties, casual in manner but intensely talkative, driving. From Milwaukee originally, he's lived in Nome the past six years, travels around to villages buying up ivory (walrus tusks, whale bone, fossil mammoth and mastodon tusks), carved and uncarved, buying it up for resale in Nome. I suspect some of the stuff he buys comes from that mound behind the village—not strictly legal trade. Eric is happy to spend $100 to get here, confident of turning a good profit in Nome.

He cuts overhead, I'm told, by bringing in booze and selling it to a few reliable customers. The night he spent here was the only time I've seen a drunken Eskimo in the village. As that old man weaved his way up the street, children were called in to their homes. Eric is also blamed for the break up last year of a marriage. Again it was booze.

But it would be wrong, I am aware, to idealize Wales and blame its problems on outsiders. The occasional drowning or hunting accident, the drinking and drugs, the too frequent suicides—these are not all imports from Nome. One hundred thirty people on a sandy spit of land reaching into an arctic sea—what a fragile enterprise at any time of year! And when winter closes in with roof-high drifts, sub-zero cold, and nearly continuous dark, who'd blame the whole town for folding up and moving elsewhere?

Wrong again. Those are my white-man's natural assumptions, but in fact not winter but summer is the alien season here. Oh, the few warm perfect days of continuous sunlight are appreciated, but except for fish-camp the residents of Wales find summer boring. There's just not much to do. The kids play soccer and climb on the roofs. The adults play pinochle, pool (in the Village Association rec hall), and visit back and forth. Winter brings snow-machines, ice-skating, downhill and cross-country skiing, dog sleds. Chop a hole in the ice and drop a line. Remembering keenly, Walter tells me how he contrived a twenty-foot-long snow tunnel from the post office door out to the street last winter. Snow is the Eskimo's element.

I'm here on a rural orientation program from the University of Alaska where I teach. Just whose orientation is involved is not exactly clear, but I dutifully pass out the stamped postcards I've been given addressed to the Office of Admissions and Records. The villagers can write for information. Natives make up about ten percent of the students at the Fairbanks campus, well below their proportion in the state population. I find, however, that the people of Wales are well aware of the University: the chairman of the Art Department, Ron Senungetuk, comes from Wales. Walter Weyapuk asks me somewhat wistfully if it's true that it takes four full years to get a degree. It's just too long to be away from the village, where he is an important member of the Council and the Board of the Village Corporation. Since the Native Claims Settlement Act, the village has had to manage large sums of money. The new general store was built out of these funds, but in general, Walter says, the older people just want the money kept in a bank. He would like to see more spent on improvements: a better generator, perhaps, or plumbing.

Besides Walter, a number of kids—teenagers—seem genuinely interested in the university. But whether interested or not, the villagers all seem puzzled by my presence. Archaeologists have been here to study their mound and anthropologists to study their traditions, their way of life, but I am neither of these. I shrug, smile, repeat the words, rural orientation, and try to explain.

One feeling I neglected to mention before, but it comes back to me strongly as I sit here on the ridge looking out over all that land and water—is privilege. What an honor to be able to fly into this village, be met at the airstrip and welcomed into a home. I pay my way of course, but that's not the point. It's so easy in this day of mass culture to lose all sense of the particularity of your own personal experience: how little we do that isn't equally available to everyone we know. But this is certainly different and enriching. My strongest regret, I find, is that I can't stay longer and spend some time at the fish-camp. The impact of Western culture is recent, subsistence hunting thousands of years old.

Yesterday, a flock of cranes in a lopsided V flew over, honking, coming from Siberia. Someone ran outside of a house and fired a shot at them right in the middle of the village. I'll take that away with me, along with all the bones that litter and for me symbolize the elemental nature of the place: whale bones, seal bones, scattered vertebrae and ribs—bones of all sizes going back to the sand. On one doorstep the skulls and tusks of half a dozen walruses.

And I'll take this—a yellow Bombi Bombardier towing a flatbed trailer. On the flatbed a green metal boat with two outboards. In the boat, brown plastic bags loaded with supplies, and four people sitting up there, two with holstered pistols. A large tan dog is handed up to them and eagerly joins their company, as they set off in high spirits for camp. One of the men in the trailer is white: someone who stayed.

I feel I could stay too, but I know I won't. A question arises. I've taken no snapshots, what can I bring home with me that will inevitably remind me of this place? The shells on the beach— some are beautiful—and the driftwood, sure I've collected some, but these are much like shells and driftwood from any beach, only more plentiful.

I know what I want. Behind the Weyapuks' house, discarded among sandgrass, there's a large whale vertebra from that bowhead they got last spring. It must be twenty inches across the beam, a rich creamy brown, and nobody seems to claim it.

The morning I'm to leave the weather turns bad. A strong southeast wind, heavy fog. The whitecaps are up. KNOM announces that a Wein Twin-Otter has taken off for Shishmaref, Wales, Teller, and back to Nome. No mention of my Forster Cessna. It seems touch and go as I lug my suitcase, my sleeping bag, my whale vertebra—I seem to need another hand for all this—out to the hanger, a quarter of a mile from town. I watch the fog and mist lift, then come back heavy. I hear a drone. It's the Twin-Otter taxiing up the runway. I'll get on it if I can. But it turns out to be mostly for freight and full-up. Then, as they're about to take off, they pass the word that's just come in by radio: my charter is on its way.

I have at least an hour's wait. My thoughts move forward and back, but already my experiences here are changing, acquiring a frame, becoming dreamlike. I don't feel I'm losing them. I feel they're going deeper. Last night I stayed up till near two a.m. and wrote most of this article—just a snapshot, really. I can't claim more for it than that. Others will have to do the sociology, the economics, the political structure of the place. They will see Wales, perhaps, as a problem to be solved, and solving it will come away with answers of a much more positive sort than any I've acquired.

What can I do? I'm just a tourist after all. I love the place, but I can't stay. Yesterday I asked Flo Weyapuk about the vertebra, whether it would be all right to take it. She shrugged and said, a bit puzzled, a bit amused: "You found it. It's yours."

SEASON OF DEAD WATER
(A Review) *

It is more than two years now since the oil spill in Prince William Sound, time enough for editorials, legal hearings and the trial of Captain Hazelwood, time enough, in other words, to start sorting out the blame. And time enough for poets and essayists to begin to reflect on and draw meaning from the disaster.

Helen Frost has gathered work by forty-four writers, among them Marvin Bell, Jean-Michel Cousteau, Wendell Berry, John Haines, Carolyn Kizer, W. S. Merwin, William Stafford and Nancy Willard, as well as others less well known, some of whom are being published for the first time. We hear the voices of Alaskans who were on the scene, of concerned citizens from other places who came to participate in the clean-up, and of those who felt the impact of the spill from a distance. The book takes its title from remarks by Walter Meganack, Sr., Chief of Port Graham village on Alaska's Kenai Peninsula: "We walk our beaches. But the snails and the barnacles and the chitons are falling off the rocks. Dead. Dead water.... We walk our beaches. But instead of gathering life, we gather death."

Though relatively short, the book is dense in emotion and in serious reflection. From these writers' varied responses to the oil spill, the reader can start to measure his or her own.

The spill of the Exxon-Valdez differs from other man-made disasters (Chernobyl, Bhopal), not in its causes—administrative errors, greed, carelessness, lack of an adequate response, etc.—but in its results, which killed many thousands of animals and birds, and

---

* *Season of Dead Water*, edited by Helen Frost. Portland, OR: Breitenbush Books, Inc., 1990.

devastated the ecology of Prince William Sound, but destroyed no human life. Thus, though in purely human terms hardly ranking as a disaster—think of recent earthquakes for contrast—it sticks in the mind and heart because it calls into question our daily actions and our long term objectives. We are all environmentalists, of course—that is until it comes to heating our houses, driving our cars, and earning our livings. The Exxon-Valdez spill gives the lie to such complacency.

On another level, the oil spill carries the force of an ancient, almost universal myth. How many times was the word "pristine" invoked to describe the beauty of Prince William Sound before the accident? And that myth has force. Listen to Kelly Weaverling (interviewed by Denita Benyshek) talk about his first impression on flying in to the sound many years before the spill: it was, he says, "paradise. When I landed in a float plane just off shore a little spit of land, there was a glacier that came to the sea, calving icebergs. There were mountains with snow all around me. Floating icebergs in the lagoon and seals and otters on them. A pod of orcas blew just in front of me. One of them had a very distinctive bent fin and I've seen him every year since 1976. I realized this was home. There was no reason for me to go anywhere else, ever again."

Not surprisingly in many of the poems, essays and stories in *Season of Dead Water*, the myth of a paradise destroyed by human greed and carelessness is evoked. It is a natural fit with the subject—a before and after the fall situation—which writers find hard to resist. One of its most subtle uses is in Christianne Balk's poem, "Before the Spill...", which simply catalogs the richness of "before," while foreshadowing the images of dying otters and oiled birds we all now carry with us.

This sea
wants everything—the black cod's eye, phalarope,
green fucus, milky clouds of milt, the otter's coat,
the shadowed cracks between each rock along this jagged
coast, sooty shearwater and steel hulled ship,

sea lions thick with pups, razor clams, pot shrimps...

Because they are "almost human" in appearance, otters are repeatedly mentioned and described in the book—particularly the young and their mothers. Inevitably, their fate attaches our emotions, as it did for those directly involved in the rescue and clean-up. Helen Frost, editor of the collection, includes a poem of her own written from the point of view of a mother otter and beginning, "Child, there was a time when we could trust/the water."

Several of the book's prose accounts of dying animals and birds are graphic and harrowing. But eventually, at the peak of the spill's spread, it was the absence of life that dominated. In a set of journal excerpts titled, "The Sound of Oil," Gary Osborne writes: "I came upon one group of six or seven seals. It seemed that half of them were oiled and very listless. I didn't attempt a close approach as I am sure they have been stressed to near, or beyond, their limits. There was no other life, no shore birds, no otters, no gulls, total silence prevailed."

Pursuing a mythic reading of the spill, if these events call up the story of the fall, bringing death into the world (and all our woe), then perhaps the devil's role is the temptation of profit (Greed) working through his agent-snake, the giant corporation—Exxon. But on reflection one might want to qualify this view. After all, otters and seals and sea birds are predators themselves and death is not something new in the natural world. Rather it's modern man's capacity, working on a huge scale, to throw nature dramatically out of balance that the spill so clearly demonstrates.

No one wanted this spill to happen, or worked to achieve it—certainly not Exxon, however badly it may have behaved, nor its agent, Captain Hazelwood. As in chaos theory, a series of small miscalculations produced horrifyingly vast consequences. This is not to say, of course, that those who made the mistakes, and who lied, and failed to follow common sense procedures, who took risks and violated laws should not be called to account: their behavior *ought* to be punished, both as an example to others and to satisfy our sense of justice.

But we should be careful that the story doesn't end there. In his essay "Tear Out Our Hearts," John Keeble notes: "The otter, the newfound Bambi...conjured up the myth of the lost garden. From this springs our melancholy regard for Alaska as the last wilderness on American soil, and this is probably what triggered the remarkable but sometimes merely sentimental and so, quickly exhausted outpouring of concern over the spill on the part of the American public."

Though some of the work here falls into the Bambi trap, most of it deals more complexly with the spill. Caught in Chicago traffic (we remember what fuel powers all those cars), hearing about the spill on her car radio, former Alaskan Patricia Monaghan writes: "There is no way now to be innocent.... There is not one of us/who was not on the bridge that night."

John Wahl, who has himself worked in oil exploration, is able to call up the voice of Joseph Hazelwood and suggest his twists of anger, self-pity, and recrimination in the face of universal calamity:

> Contempt goes down smooth, sure it does,
> a sippin' whiskey from the top shelf;
> I'd be honored, except that you're merely drunkards,
> so bottom's up and go to hell...
> Perhaps my only peace of mind was found
> while watching otters and sea birds,
> a glacier breathing vigor into my exhausted face...
> Does it matter at journey's end? O captain
> my Captain, we held a hummingbird's heart
> carelessly between our teeth
> and crushed the Earth with a shrug.

If the poems and journal entries bring our emotions about the spill back—and who could read them without experiencing moments of powerful grief?—a number of the essays in Frost's collection raise the issues to an impressive level of argument and speculation. After we contemplate the myth of the spill and share out the blame, we must try to derive some lesson and some plan of action, so that similar disasters can be prevented in the future. (Heaven forbid that we should be left helpless in the face of giant corporations and human carelessness!)

Charles Konigsberg describes Exxon's attempt to control the terms of the debate during the clean-up: "Numbers of people, lengths of boom, miles of coast, numbers and size of boats and the like.... Numbers-dollars-things automatically...diverts attention and concern from the cultural and ecological, life-threatening dimension of this tragic catastrophe, while also fostering dissension and conflict."

Anthropologist Richard Nelson carries the argument forward: "We belong to a society much like the tanker in Prince William Sound, laden with an enormous deadly cargo, making its way through treacherous waters with impaired judgment at the helm." Reflecting on who'll pay for the spill, Nelson concludes, "We will cover the cost to government when we pay taxes. We will cover the cost to the oil industry when we buy fuel or anything made with petroleum products. The notion that someone else will pay is an illusion."

The more you think about it, the deeper the problem becomes, for it is not a question of numbers, but of how we choose to live. Wendell Berry tackles this issues in his essay "Word and Flesh": "It was not just the greed of corporate shareholders and the hubris of corporate executives that put the fate of Prince William Sound into one ship; it was also our demand that energy be cheap and plentiful. The economies of our communities and households are wrong." And he goes on: "We must achieve the character and acquire the skills to live much poorer than we do. We must waste less. We must do more for ourselves and each other. It is either that or continue merely to think and talk about changes that we are inviting catastrophe to make."

Berry sees bigness as the enemy: "Nature...is plainly saying to us, 'If you put the fates of whole communities or cities or regions or ecosystems at risk in single ships or factories or power plants, then I will furnish the drunk or the fool or the imbeciles who will make the necessary small mistake.'" Though he carries his argument through impressively from first principles, Berry's solution is utopian. We must move into small self-sufficient communities that take care of their own production and deal with their own waste. It seems unlikely that many can follow his lead, yet he may well be right to say, "We are not smart enough or conscious enough or alert enough to work responsibly on a gigantic scale."

Of course for Berry's solution to succeed against such potential catastrophes as global warming it has to be applied on a global scale, with ecologically-minded rural communities flourishing while cities are abandoned. It seems too unlikely to hope for, but perhaps Nature has further surprises in store for us that will force such an outcome.

◁

John Keeble cites as a prevailing opinion "that [the Sound's] populations, the otters, birds and intertidal life will recover, and that the thousand miles of damaged beaches will eventually finish 'cleaning themselves.' Some put the recovery time at three years. Others put it at twenty-five."

Charles Wohlforth who visited the scene late last year [1990] calls this into question. "Leaving oil in the environment, to weather and dilute, to bleed out of beaches and poison seashore life, was called, 'letting nature clean it up.' If you can't buy a happy ending, call the tragic ending by another name....

"'Letting nature clean it up' was an especially ironic phrase in Kodiak. While Prince William Sound cleaned itself, Kodiak, downstream in the prevailing currents, got dirtier all summer. Beaches were being freshly hit by oil as Exxon was pulling out in September.

"Standing on the beaches of Kodiak and the Alaska Peninsula, I felt like I was standing at the edge of the world. The Shelikof Strait's unreliable horizon was a soft, smudged pencil line, losing itself in equally gray sky like an erasure at the edge of a map. Oil blobs were at my feet. Nature 'cleans' itself by spreading the oil ever farther. That kind of 'clean' is complete when every beach is equally dirty."

Season of Dead Water is a disturbing book, as it should be. It brings our feelings about the spill close once again, and offers a wide range of reflection and response that gives the reader much to think about. But, unless one accepts Wendell Berry's utopian vision with everyone moving into small, self-sufficient communities, it offers no final answer. As the memory of the spill recedes, the call goes out from most of Alaska's politicians to open the Arctic Wildlife Refuge to oil drilling, while in the Middle East armies continue to gather and contest the ownership of the wells.

TALES FROM THE DENA
(A Review)*

It's mid-July as I write, and here in interior Alaska it won't get dark for another month. But by late November we'll have only a few hours of sun, and that season of the long nights, as the Native peoples of Alaska know, is a good time for telling stories.

In Frederica de Laguna's introduction to her collection of Koyukon Indian tales, the distinguished anthropologist explains that "in the most bitter cold of December and early January little fishing or hunting is attempted, and in the cramped quarters of the winter houses, illuminated during the long dark hours only by the open fire and the small clay lamps of fish oil, the Koyukon wait for spring, or, with the lights extinguished, listen while some storyteller 'bites off a piece of the winter' with a myth of 'Distant Time.'"

Interior Alaska is a big place. John McPhee once said that if you stole Italy and were looking for a place to stash it where it wouldn't be noticed for a while, the middle of Alaska would be a good spot. When the Russians first immigrated here in the 1830s, they found scattered communities of seventy, eighty, or, at most, a few hundred Dena (as the Native people call themselves) living along the Yukon River and its tributaries. With them, the Russians brought smallpox, which reduced the population further. Between 1847 and 1848, L. A. Zogoskin estimated the number of Yukon and Kuskokwim River Natives at about fifteen hundred, which is probably too low. By 1934, the population of Athabaskan Indians

---

* *Tales From the Dena: Indian Stories from the Tanana, Koyukuk, and Yukon Rivers,* edited by Frederica de Laguna and illustrated by Dale DeArmond. Seattle: University of Washington Press, 1996.

in the interior—excluding those who had moved into the cities—numbered only about five hundred.

In 1935, Frederica de Laguna led a small archaeological expedition to this region, looking for early Indian sites. Their search for "old things" took them to Native villages on the Tanana, Koyukuk, and Yukon Rivers, where they had the opportunity to collect ethnographic information and to record these forty-one tales, most of them quite brief. With her colleague Norman Reynolds, de Laguna recorded a dozen different Native tellers. When several versions of the same story occur, the details and tone often differ substantially. Some of the tellers emphasize magical powers and shamanism while others stress humor or practical survival issues. Often, the origin of a particular custom or animal behavior or the name of a local landmark is illuminated. Published for the first time, the tales are grouped by location and teller, and between the fascinating seventy-page introduction and the helpful commentary at the end, they form the meat of this very generous sandwich.

Many of the stories deal with Crow—the archetypal creator and trickster known more commonly today as Raven. In one tale, Crow tracks a rival chief to the far end of the world and tricks him into giving back the sun, which he'd stolen. De Laguna presents four different versions of this important story. In one, Crow is given payment in food for bringing the sun back, linking the crucial issues of hunger and light for the Dena. In another tale, hunger drives Crow to kill and eat his hunting companion, Whale; and in one of the strangest stories in the collection, the famished Crow pulls out his own guts and eats them.

A second major group of tales deals with the Traveler, called in one version "The Man Who Went through Everything." The Traveler's stories begin with his childhood, when he proves incompetent at all the tasks his widowed mother sets out for him. Through ignorance and foolishness, he fails at setting traps for rabbits, catching fish and porcupines, and even cutting down trees. No task is too simple for him not to bungle, and we may assume his comic ineptitude was amusing to the children who listened, drawing them into the saga. But once the Traveler ventures out on his own, he becomes a quick learner and an innovator. He studies different kinds of bark to determine which floats best, then invents the first canoe and travels down the Yukon, encountering the many creatures who inhabit this land and overcoming obstacles, both natural and human. According to storyteller Eliza Jones, his mission was to correct all the things that were wrong in the world. A complete telling of the Traveler's story cycle is said to take eight nights.

The book's seventy-three woodblock illustrations by Alaskan artist Dale DeArmond imaginatively capture the spirit of the tales and help the reader appreciate them more fully. In one important respect the illustrations are crucial; de Laguna informs us that in 1935, "crow" was the English word universally used by natives for the larger, much more impressive raven. In point of fact, there are no crows in interior Alaska but ravens are common. Thus, DeArmond's prints make clear what the storytellers obviously had in mind, allowing the reader to see that inventive and powerful, but often devious creature fishing fire from the river, sitting on the bones of Whale, and courting and then killing Willow Grouse. Sometimes rumpled and defeated, at other times sleek in triumph, the sly Raven creator is beautifully present in the book thanks to DeArmond.

A casual reader might be tempted to jump right into the tales without dwelling on de Laguna's introductory material, but that would be a mistake. It's important to have some sense of the harsh life and rich traditional culture these stories reflect; however, it isn't easy to travel across cultures, and even with all of de Laguna's help, puzzles remain. For example, when Crow kills and eats his hunting companion, Whale, how should this be understood? Is it permissible under extreme circumstances to take such liberties? Surely not. The clue is in the tale itself: Crow is ashamed of what he's done and tries unsuccessfully to hide it; yet the story tells us something of the brutal conditions these northern hunters faced and describes the unacceptable thoughts that hunger can suggest.

A Dena child heard these tales many times and was expected to ponder them and draw different meanings at different ages. For the youngest listeners, the pure narrative and the amazing magical qualities of the world in the stories must have made a strong impression. Older children would have seen that the tales also offer practical instructions for survival and illuminate the customs of the Koyukon; for example, they explain how the three clans originated and why certain social behaviors are expected.

Sometimes these points are difficult to grasp across the barriers of time and culture. Why, for instance, should a hunter never directly name the animal he is going after? This may sound like a mere superstition, but it is much more than that, reflecting a belief system in which all living things can easily communicate and a careless comment is sure to be passed along. To name your prey is a kind of bragging and shows disrespect, and no caribou, moose, or rabbit will consent to be killed unless it is treated with utmost respect. Beneath the surface, then, these tales carry lessons that, even today, adults need to keep in mind and measure their actions against.

There are more Koyukons in rural Alaska today than when de Laguna collected these stories, but the Native languages are dying out and the survival of the culture is in question. However, for several weeks each summer, across the Tanana River from where I live, tents go up around the substantial log house of Howard Luke, a distinguished Native elder. I wondered about those gatherings, then learned from a friend of Howard's that they were "spirit camps," where the local traditions are being taught to a new generation.

Tales from the Dena provides a rich introduction to the world of these northern hunters. Their culture, although modified through contact with our own, still survives in this harsh and magical landscape.

A DENALI JOURNAL

When I told my writer friends that I was going to be writer-in-residence at Denali National Park and that if things went well, this might become a regular thing like the artist-in-residence program they have there each summer, everyone had the same reaction: *don't screw up!*

I spent 10½ days at the East Fork Cabin, aka the "Murie Cabin" on the East Fork of the Toklat River, near Polychrome Pass. It's furnished with a double bunk bed, a propane stove and refrigerator, and has impressive bear-proof shutters with long rusty nails sticking out to discourage break-ins. (I'm told that bears like to scratch their backs on the nails.)   Built as the local headquarters for the construction crew on the park road, the cabin is best known for the fact that the naturalist Adolph Murie lived there in the early 1940s while studying Denali's wolves. The location couldn't be more central,   43 miles from the park entrance and about the same distance from Wonder Lake at the far end. I had free run of the park road with my formerly green, now very dusty-brown, Subaru, and I quickly learned that whatever you plan or expect, something else, something quite amazing will likely turn up.

I had been to the park many times before, but on this visit I felt from the start that something extraordinary was happening. Being "in residence" means, in a sense, being at home, and having the wonderful Murie Cabin to live in made me feel a part of the wilderness whenever I stepped outside. The philosopher William James has written that one of the basic qualities of a mystical experience is that it cannot be captured in words. He may be right, but I felt I had to try. It was unlike anything that had ever happened to me before.

DAY 1 (June 19, 2009). Driving in to the cabin, I saw a group of 14 caribou being pestered by a pair of long-tailed jaegers—move along, move along!—they swooped and shouted, protesting the intrusion on their territory. Focusing my binocs, I accidentally hit the car horn with my elbow and all the caribou stopped dead and looked around for the source of the noise. I thought, "Strike one, for me."

Perched on the cabin porch as I arrived, a resident ground squirrel, with cupped ears and stubby tail, came to rigid attention, sizing me up.

After moving my gear into the 14' x 16' cabin, I heard some loud talk and laughter coming from down toward the East Fork River. Kennen and Karen Ward—naturalist filmmakers—and a pair of park interpreters were watching some fox kits poke their heads out of the den holes and peak from over the top of the hill. As we observed them watching us, we talked about how, if you're patient, if you're willing to stand around and wait, something interesting will eventually reveal itself. A day or two before, the Kennens had come upon a lynx sitting on the branch of a tree, patiently waiting for a meal to wander by underneath.

While eating my dinner—some chicken cacciatore, which Nancy had cooked and frozen for me—I read what earlier cabin residents had written in the log book set out on the table, and found myself suddenly moved to tears, feeling a rush of assent at one of the artists' comments: "It's as if you dropped me off in Paradise."

DAY 2. Scanning with binocs at the river, a dark rock-like thing on the ridge-line across the river and past the East Fork Bridge turned out to be a golden eagle, profiled against the blue sky and looking regal. Every once in a while it turned its head, scanning off into the distance and after about ten minutes, two other eagles circled in. Seen straight on, the wings practically disappeared in the blue haze, making them look like shadowy ghost-birds.

After lunch I took a bus to the Eielson Visitor's Center, about twenty miles west of the cabin. On the ride I sat next to a talkative guy who reminded me of my late father-in-law—something about the sharp angles of his face and the assertive way he talked. But when I mentioned that I'm a poet, he brightened up: "Oh, I love poetry!" and named a poet he's been reading lately, a woman I'd never heard of who writes religious verse. I was almost sorry I'd brought the subject up, but he went on to explain that what he liked about her poetry was the way she could express fresh ideas—things you'd never think of yourself—in clear and memorable language. Not a bad tribute.

The new Eielson was new to me, smaller than I'd expected, and designed to fit into the landscape. It holds an impressive collection of resident artists' work, with a beautiful wall-size quilt by Ree Nancarrow tracking the seasons in the park prominently displayed. Now we'll have to get some writers in there too.

DAY 3. Drove to Tattler Creek and hiked in through willows ringing my bear bells—not to attract them of course but to warn them off. Found the side-canyon where a couple of geology students recently discovered some dinosaur footprints and took a photo of what may be one—though it isn't the common three-toed kind. On the drive back, I saw a mother ptarmigan and two tiny checks crossing the road. I pulled over and heard her motherly peepings hurrying them along.

On this trip I find that my interest in bears and moose is somewhat less but my interest in the smaller creatures grows: my neighbor foxes, the rabbits who nibble leaves and grasses near the cabin, and the ground squirrel family who den under the porch and are eager to become friends or at least get a handout. I'm also watching some recently fledged baby magpies who hop and flutter around in the low spruce trees near the river.

Also, perhaps thanks to the artists who've painted them, I find myself responding more fully to the landscapes of the park. Not just the spectacle of Mt. McKinley, but more locally. The smaller mountains seen from this cabin window, for instance, with dots and streaks of snow, the looping green and brown hills rising to snow-splashed peaks, with shifting clouds and cloud-shadows, rabbits and magpies hopping and flitting in the foreground. No bears here yet.

DAY 4. After showering at the staff washhouse at Toklat, I continued out to Eielson and hiked above the visitor center. The wildflowers were amazing—such varieties of colors and shape, the alpine forget-me-nots an incredible neon blue. On the drive back I saw the Ward's camper pulled over and their camera set up. A sow grizzly and two 1st year cubs—tiny by comparison—foraged in the middle distance. She's blond and they're both brown and when she lay back for them to nurse I had to try for a picture, though it was probably too far for my camera. The Wards complained about a tour bus driver, who, after they'd spent a long time setting up for the shoot, pulled in and made them move their stuff. It seemed like gratuitous rank-pulling because there were plenty of other spots along the road where the bears could be seen from the bus.

While in the park, I'm reading Robert Richardson's fine book on Thoreau (*Henry Thoreau: A Life of the Mind*). It turns out that Thoreau experienced true wilderness not at Walden Pond—a short stroll from his home in Concord—but rather on Mt. Katahdin in northern Maine, where, alone in howling wind, surrounded by barren rock, feeling sick and worn-out, he encountered a nature that was in no way hospitable to our species. He realized that nature has a range of experiences to offer and concluded that in essence there isn't just one nature, but two. The familiar one, almost domestic, offers a healing relief from the petty distractions and restrictions of human communities, but, at the other end of its range, lies a hostile, barren world, which he called "Demonic Nature." Thoreau felt that this harsh and alien environment was also important to humans, because, as he wrote, "We need to witness our own limits transgressed."

And reading this, I realized that at the present time, while I'm relaxing in the cabin or cruising up and down the park road, picking from a menu of easy to moderate hikes, there are climbers taking on Mt. McKinley itself, voluntarily putting their lives at risk, testing their limits and in some cases having their limits transgressed.

DAY 5. A little after one a.m., the excited barkings of a young fox gets me out of bed. I see it dashing toward the den, pause and bark as if calling for a parent or sib, then turn and race back into the brush where it continues to bark as I write this. A first kill perhaps? The look on its face—a mixture of terror and pride—as if its young life had come upon something utterly new and amazing. Its bark—not like a dog's—could be mistaken for a crow cawing—as I did at first—but the barks are longer than caws and the silence between more spread out. Foxes are usually thought of as quiet and stealthy, but this one has something to crow about.

Its excitement reminds me of my own childhood—some great discovery going way back, learning to walk, or speaking my first complete sentence. Or later on, as a sixth grader, belting a softball over the right fielder's head. And in a way it also connects to the present moment, to the honor I feel in having this residency.

Straightened the cabin and with some difficulty made the upper bunk, since Nancy and Ben will be spending the next few days here. Then I walked along the gravel toward the East Fork Bridge, to see if we could get under and explore to the north, but a solid rock-face blocks the way. Going, I saw a fragment of a small animal part—possibly the leg of a rabbit—and coming back the fresh prints of what I took to be a young moose and another creature, the second one having hand-sized paws with five claw-marks, so possibly a small bear. They seemed to be in contact, which I read as a pursuit, but which in the Disney version would be featured as a cross-species buddy movie.

I drove to the Savage River to meet Nancy and Ben who were coming out by bus, and to pass the time till their arrival climbed the steep pinnacle on the Savage Rock Trail. Starting down I took the wrong route and could have gotten myself in serious trouble, but another climber corrected me. Getting straightened around took some serious (for me at 65!) rock climbing. I remembered my catastrophic fall 50 years ago in New Mexico and felt pretty stupid for getting myself into this mess, but by focusing on making one small move at a time—and not looking down!—I got myself back on the trail.

DAY 6. Woke up to heavy rain, low clouds and not much prospect for change, but hey—this is the park! So we drove west, hoping for something different, and we got it—snow. Heading over Polychrome, rain turned to sleet and we could see the snow-level on the mountains dropping. The road wasn't bad, though, and we continued out to Eielson, seeing along the way a mother grizzly playing in the snow with her single cub. They wrestled and rolled around in the frosty white stuff, delighted with each other, and turned on by the snow.

At Eielson we walked into a snowball fight involving some visiting kids and the bus dispatcher. He took shelter in his office fort, making gleeful forays out to return fire. Fog and snow shifted around us on our walk and we had only scattered glimpses of the massive peaks nearby. On the way back, snow having let up, we hiked near Stoney Creek and came on a fresh-looking pile of bear scat and, nearby, a stretch of ripped up ground where the bear apparently went after a ground squirrel. Seeing a few square yards of earth gouged and torn apart, big rocks tossed aside like ping-pong balls—a thorough thrashing of the region—gave a new and very different perspective (different from the playful wrestling of a mother and cub) of the wild power and menace of a bear. We proceeded no further.

DAY 7. We hiked at Tattler Creek, noting wildflowers and ringing for bears. The creek gets its name from the wandering tattler, a rare bird that breeds here. We saw no bears, but unfortunately, we saw no wandering tattlers either. I hiked into the rugged side-canyon, looking for more dinosaur footprints, and saw many possible maybes, but no definite prints.

We crossed the stream and climbed to an open spot where we could see lots of Dall sheep. A film-maker was carrying his camera and tripod up-slope to get himself into position to shoot them. Hunters of this sort are common in the park, but no guns are permitted, not till November when, thanks to the NRA, the rules will change. At that point the park will become less wild and more dangerous. *

We ate lunch on a flowery hill with excellent views of sheep hanging out where the high tundra meets the rock. On the way back, we had to make another crossing of Tattler Creek. Following Nancy, I noticed that one of the rocks she stepped on had shifted slightly, so I was careful in placing a foot on it, but it shifted again, throwing me off balance. I've asked her if I could write that I "fell gracefully into the stream." She replied: "You can say that if you like, but it would be a lie."

On my hands and knees in three inches of icy water, I took stock.

---

* Early in 2010, for the first time in park history, a visitor shot and killed a grizzly bear, claiming self-defense. The shooting took place near Tattler Creek.

A few minor scrapes, I thought, nothing big. But something was wrong with my left pinky. It looked like a miniature hacksaw, with the middle section out of line. It hurt quite a bit too. I figured I might have to drive to the clinic in Healy outside the park to have it put right, but as we were hiking out, I fiddled with the joint, and it slipped back into place. The pain quickly subsided.

As we drove back to the cabin, at the far end of Sable Pass, Mt. McKinley was beautifully out, both summits sharp and clear, towering over the nearby hills. Though we'd been to the park many times, this impressive view was new to us.

DAY 8. Nancy and Ben packed up to go and we drove to the Teklanika campground and hiked alternately through the woods and along the gravel bars of the river. Moose sign and the tracks of (possibly) a wolf. We ate our lunch sandwiches out on a bar, then headed for the park entrance. On the way we saw a big moose cross the road. I stopped just as another even bigger male jogged across and moved off into the trees.

I dropped Nancy and Ben at their car, gassed up and drove back to the cabin.

DAY 9. Today I was scheduled to drive out to North Fork Lodge in Kantishna at the far end of the park for a reading.

An elderly fox meandered ahead of me on the road as I headed up toward Polychrome Pass. Red smudged, with black along its sides and with ribs showing it wasn't the handsomest of foxes. Pausing, it rubbed its muzzle on a scrap of something—perhaps some former meal—at the side of the road, not paying any attention to the car that followed impatiently on its tail.

Then, approaching the overlook, something amazing. Sun shearing through low clouds transformed the view to glitter, everything golden, scintillant, and as the road crested over its top, reality shifted toward vision. I felt transformed myself and checked my shaky hands on the steering wheel. But in my euphoria it seemed that if I went over the edge nothing very bad would happen. Physical and temporal boundaries dissolved. It was unlike anything I'd ever experienced and felt like a culmination not just of this residency, but of everything in my life leading up to it. That intense, magical feeling lasted for about fifteen minutes, but it continued to reverberate through the day.

At Thoroughfare, where I expected the grizzly family (brown cubs, blond mother), instead—to my astonishment—a caribou herd, well over 100 of them, grazed and moved gradually west toward Eielson. Lots of young ones, with four of them lined up in a game of "follow the leader," their herd instinct already at work.

After a brief visit to Camp Denali, where we'd stayed for a couple of days in 1977 when Jeff was one year old (now he's a poet too, living in Brooklyn), I showered at North Face Lodge and then met up with a poet who was working on the staff. At 69, Jill Carter had come out from Massachusetts for the summer to experience Alaska. She was delighted to have another poet on the premises and talked up my reading to the other staff members. I had dinner with the guests and told them about my residency, after which the reading went very well. Lots of smart questions afterwards.

Driving back to the cabin late, I gave an involuntary shout of surprise at a stunning double rainbow flowing upward from the base of Mt. McKinley. Brilliant colors, with the muscular shoulders of the mountain behind it, topped by thick dark clouds.

Toward midnight nearing Eielson, I ran into the Wards again. Since there's only one road through the park, these meetings are fated rather than coincidental. They told me that earlier in the day they'd seen some wolves take a caribou calf from the herd I'd been watching. After their meal, the pack had divided up the remaining parts and carried them back to the den-site.

Day 10. At an early hour, before I was properly into the day, I heard a car door slam, then another, and two voices speaking in a foreign tongue approached the cabin. I hurried to the door.

"Hello?" There stood two men in slacks and turtleneck sweaters, glancing at each other, apparently unsure how to respond. One of them grinned sheepishly and the other muttered, "Murie... Murie..."

Finally, a third person, white bearded and bespectacled, stepped forward and raised an arm in greeting. "These are two wolf specialists from Spain," he said. "I thought they should see the cabin."

"Oh, sure," I said, stepping aside, and at that the two Spaniards rushed past me and scurried about, excitedly taking note of my papers, books, and clothes scattered about and exclaiming, "Murie! Murie!" And when they soon departed, I felt I had served the cause of international wolf studies, though, sad to say, I haven't seen a single wolf myself during this particular stay in the park.

DAY 11. My last morning in the cabin, I went down to the river to have a last look around and while I was casually staring at the thick gray fast-flowing channel, a head poked up mid-stream. What kind of head? I couldn't tell. It was gone too quickly. Had it been a fish, trying to get its bearings? A river otter? Maybe it was just a trick of light on the riffles. Had I really seen anything at all?

But then in almost the exact same place, the head poked up again, this time followed by the long neck and mottled body of a duck—I couldn't tell what kind. And at once it was paddling desperately toward the bank, and seemed about to make it, when it disappeared again under the silty current. I scrambled over to the spot where it would have come out if it had reached the shore, but there was no duck there.

MOVING TO FAIRBANKS:
NOTES ON POETRY AND PLACE

It's 1976, and Pan Am still has direct jet service from New York. We get on the plane at Kennedy, and seven and a half hours later we pass over the zigzag pipeline snaking across the tundra and land in Fairbanks. It could be anywhere on the globe. We have no feeling of having traveled to a particular place, no sense of a difficult journey, obstacles overcome, a passage, a goal achieved. For a poet this is surely the wrong way to do it, but we're modern people, we're mobile, and we expect the convenience of jet travel when we want to get to anyplace far-off.

Moving to Alaska was easy, being Alaskan harder. Over thirty years later, I've seen only a fraction of this vast state, but I've built my house here, learned to ski cross-country, and one winter I changed three flat tires at minus fifty. I have to admit, though, the New York I brought with me still makes me, in a sense, a New York poet. The twenty-first century is too far advanced in me for any easy nostalgia for Robert Service.

The other day, as I shoveled out the mailboxes along with my neighbor, a German electrician—the one who wired my house— we paused after every few shovelfuls and looked out on the frozen Tanana River, where skiers and snow-machiners cavorted. Occasionally you see dog sleds out there too, and in summer several stern-wheelers ply the river with their cargo of tourists.

Beyond the river: a hundred vacant miles of low spruce and then the Alaska Range, mountains that rise to thirteen, fourteen thousand feet, and—visible on the way out from town, though not from here—is Mount McKinley, at twenty thousand feet, the highest point in North America. Though mid-February, it was thirty above, and we shoveled in down vests and shirtsleeves.

I came here vowing to myself not to appropriate too casually what was not, after all, my native material. I had it in mind to hold back and live here a while before writing about anything Alaskan. I stuck to that resolution for about two weeks. I couldn't help myself, so much was new and interesting. Within a month I'd written a poem and an article about my first days in Fairbanks. Though other people have liked the poem, I distrust it because it seemed to come too quickly. But in a way, I suppose I'd been preparing to write that poem for a long time. Seven years earlier I'd written another poem which seems to me now to foreshadow what moving to Alaska means in a sense deeper than geography:

THE TWENTY-SIX YEARS WAR

Where is the land beyond landscape?
Slipping across the border
distant herds of snow.

Leaving the map behind, with its
diagrammed cities, four-square
musics, and all that predictable violence,

here clouds become ideas, as black
as headlines, and even less discreet.

I am learning a language
of otters and elk,
of distances
and profound insecurities.

Why do we kid ourselves?
Where teeth rot and stars fail, even sex
is a perpetual war with the dying.

Here the stone
seashell is my mother, I do not deny
it, here I am open, alone
advancing into the sky.

From Belle Harbor, where I spent my first four and a half years, you could see in the night sky the reflected glow of Manhattan. It was less than ten miles away as the crow flies, and I remember a dream I had more than once about that glowing place, a city of pleasure and light. It was a fairy-tale city, constructed of children's blocks piled magically high, and it was the first place that impressed me deeply enough to become a subject of writing.

Later, in New Rochelle, a singularly moderate and—to me—uninteresting suburb, I remember another magical place, a railway cut down below street level, with a station that had belonged to the Putnam Line (defunct) of the New York Central. There were no tracks there anymore, no booths or benches, though the ladies' room—a dark alcove without door, toilets or sink—could still be explored in its damp, crumbling state. The station was an exciting, even daring spot for me in those curious preadolescent years.

These two examples from my childhood could stand for many others. I'm sure everyone carries these special, magical places around at a deep level. For writers they are a payload, there to be mined for the precious ore they bear.

But what happens when we grow up? Do places lose that special power, that charge they have for us as children?

It's not that the character of places changes, obviously, but that we ourselves change. Our education makes us practical, but in the process we lose something, some capacity to explore ourselves through place. Other things take precedence. At the most banal level, we choose a house on the basis of what school district it's in and give up the woods or the railway cut that might have had more meaning for us and our kids than the entire curriculum of the fifth grade. In the effort to be sensible, mature adults, we overlook the emotional or spiritual powers that lie about us.

For there is a spiritual component to place, something our less mobile ancestors were more attuned to. But basic human nature hasn't changed, and if you open yourself to it, a certain locale can get into you, can lodge itself deeply in your mental world. Then, if you are a writer, it will become a natural setting for your work.

But this magical connection with a specific place doesn't ensure that the writing will be good. I once drafted a novel based on a summer I'd spent fossil-hunting in Wyoming. Great material, I thought. And I found that I could write endlessly about the landscape—the fields and orchards bleeding into badland, the buttes and canyons, the storms brewing high up in the mountains, the mountains themselves, and the sky, hundreds of miles wide. In fact, my draft gave altogether too much of that landscape and not enough of something else—character, tension, drama. Without the landscape there would have been no impulse to write, but that in itself did not make the writing good. Later I went over that material and found whole chapters becoming paragraphs as I tried to reduce the novel to what I simply could not leave out. Pushing the process further, I took what seemed the strongest paragraphs and worked them into a poem.

This is certainly not the most economical way to write: pages and pages out of which only a few details survive. But there is a benefit. The writing process teaches you what details are really essential. Better to start with the welter of life than with some bloodless abstraction.

Several winters ago my family and I drove a hundred and fifty miles northeast from Fairbanks over frozen tundra through blowing snow to the town of Central. On the way, a flock of winter-white ptarmigan crossed the road. Only their black eye-spots showed up against the snow, dots blurring and dancing, like watching TV in its early interference-plagued days—like that, but also strange beyond description to see those eye-spots lifting and hovering, vaguely attached to the white-on-white of hundreds of chicken-sized birds.

From Central we made our way to Circle Hot Springs, where a 1930's vintage hotel set among low spruce draws local visitors to its large, open-air swimming pool. Here, in minus-ten-degree cold, we swam comfortably. The hot springs provides water at over 100 degrees Fahrenheit, too hot, where it enters the pool, for swimmers to linger. Mid-pool, you can loll comfortably on a black inner tube in eighty- to ninety-degree warmth, while evaporating water condenses over your head and falls as tiny flakes of snow.

No writer can fail to be influenced, and many are overpowered, by the beauty and strangeness of this huge state.

More than half the population of Alaska is urban, though you might never guess this from the poetry we produce. Perhaps it's because our cities, like other cities, are hard to love. I suspect it is also because cities by their very nature are difficult to come to grips with, though that is one of the tasks modern poetry—from Whitman to Frank O'Hara—has set itself.

Nature is our nature, always. We are usually alone in it. We are its consciousness. In nature we expand, we become mountains, glaciers, and rivers; we encounter the other in its purest form— bear, moose, hawk, raven, mosquito.

In cities we are only one of many. Tall buildings cramp us, wall us into a narrow grid of possibilities, a grid inhabited by thousands of others like us. Instead of expanding, we are fractured, becoming many. It is like a hall of mirrors giving back oneself in a grotesque multitude. In plate-glass storefront windows this reflection is literal.

Nature offers us clear pools where we can gaze at our own image undistracted as we wait for a fish to nibble at our hook, but in cities it is not acceptable; we must glance surreptitiously, as we are hurried along by the crowd, to see that our dress is appropriate, our hair in place. We feel judged, slightly embarrassed, and we can't trust our own natural impulses.

That's one aspect of the city. Another is that it changes all too rapidly. Buildings are torn down and new ones take their places; stores close, move a few blocks, and reopen under new management; whole neighborhoods go to seed. And the city's boundaries keep shifting. Meanwhile, over there the mountains remain the same, stable, enduring only the seasons, and returning always to their former state.

If nature is of God, cities are unquestionably man-made. They are planned, of course, but whatever people plan and execute is full of error and accident. How can poetry deal with the accidental and the botched? Even a dying tree is perfect in its dying. Nothing about a city is perfect. That wonderful little restaurant— you know the one—where they have a few tables out on the sidewalk and usually a jazz group or folk singer, and great food: oh, that was last year. Now they've gone over to hard rock, added a bar, shut down the kitchen; you can probably still get a sandwich.

For some people this flux means, paradoxically, that cities are alive, vital, organic. Nature, by contrast, is static, dull. "If you've seen one mountain or moose, you've seen 'em all," was what my mother, who lived on Eighth Street in Greenwich Village, said on her one visit to Fairbanks.

Interestingly, in Alaska, the moose have adapted to the cities. They cross the expressway to invade gardens. Sometimes in winter they bed down under the big spruce in our backyard. Alaska is pipelines across mountain ranges and floatplanes on tundra lakes. It's log cabins with outhouses on downtown city streets. Alaskan cities still display their frontier roots and even the wilderness doesn't always keep its distance: occasionally bears and even caribou—though not residents like moose—visit their former territories. On a recent fall migration, one unfortunate caribou got its antlers tangled in a friend's clothesline. Last summer we slowed, then stopped, as a huge beaver dragged itself across Chena Pump Road. Foxes on the bike paths, porcupines in the backyard, eagles circling above the river. Even a fluffed-up chickadee checking out the bird feeder at minus forty can make you feel this place is pretty wild after all. What is special about Alaska is its mix of the urban and the wild without that Death Valley of suburbs in between.

I teach in the graduate writing program at the University of Alaska Fairbanks. Most of our students come from out of state. Many came here for the challenge of it and, as I did, for a sense of something distinctive in their lives. Some are born travelers, having been previously to Africa, India, New Zealand. Others had never been outside their home regions before. A letter of application from a southern California woman announced, "I've always dreamt of living in Alaska. I'm sure it's my fate."

When I got out of college over forty years ago, somebody was doing a survey on the graduating class. They wanted to know what I imagined my life would be like in ten years. Did I plan to live in the city, the suburbs? Did I expect to marry? How many children? I said I never planned to marry but to have dozens of children. I would live in the city—preferably Manhattan—or else way out in the country. The one place I didn't want to settle was where I was living right at that moment—in the suburbs. For me city and country are complementary, and I'll be delighted if some airline goes ahead and reinstitutes direct nonstop service between Fairbanks and Kennedy. Incidentally, six months after answering that questionnaire, I got married.

Although I'd been writing for years, I'd never consciously written about a place I was then living until I bought a house in rural New York State. I'm sure it had as much to do with my inner development as with outer circumstances. Living in that big old farmhouse, I found that writing about the details of my environment was a way of placing myself. Perhaps it's that the self seeks its own image in the world: a willed reflection. By the time I moved to Alaska, I'd caught the habit. A few years ago I composed a twelve poem sequence called "Above the Tanana," one poem a month, each set at the same location, a ledge overlooking the Tanana River with a view south to the Alaska Range—the same one I see from my mailbox. Since I know that descriptions of landscape by themselves can be boring, each poem in the sequence is dedicated to an important person or a group (or, in one case, a dog) in my life and the poems meditate on these relationships. The first poem written was "May"—for my wife.

ABOVE THE TANANA: MAY

for Nancy

Here are the pasques, those
purple-arising yellow-hearted flowers

brave as spring. And far below,
a duck, small bursts of wing-power

motoring along. Perched on a root above
the slough, we watch the melt of ice

flow west, a tent of wood that piles
on a bar, a dark bird looping larklike

down—so artless, unintended
like that kiss to which our lips

were given twenty years ago. There
on the banks of an urban river

I fixed you in my heart and you
were young as tenderness itself.

A raven passing overhead: he chortles,
caws, and sings, coaxing his mate

along. I add them to my list. Birds
to what purpose? Seeds of a garden

rooted in the mind. I knew when I
first saw you, I could outwait the facts.

Now, where mountains, sharp and white,
are rimmed with sky, where river ripples

stipple dark and light, here on this
shelf—hushed, we can almost hear

the tune the earth is singing to itself.

Of course not everything I write comes in response to my immediate environment, and I'm happy that it doesn't. I want my writing to take in the range of imaginative experience, to address the issues of history, of the arts, and of personal relationships. But it would be much poorer if it could not include the place that is nearest at hand—rural or urban—the most profound use of which is as a metaphor for the self in its deepest, meditative self-knowing. All places used in this way are mythological and reach between people, across decades, across continents.